Adopted

Adopted

Loss, love, family and reunion

Jo Willis & Brigitta Baker

MASSEY UNIVERSITY PRESS

To Lawrie, my rock, and a constant
source of love through the fog.
To Will and Hollie, I am so proud of who
you have become, and so grateful to you
both for mirroring back to me my best
parts and loving me despite my worst.
I love you all this much …
with my whole heart.

JW

To Zoë and Jade, who have been able to grow
up in a country where young women are
no longer pressured to give up their babies,
and to Andrew, who held my hand through
the entire journey.

BB

CONTENTS

Foreword	6
Prologue	9
Introduction	11

PART 1: *Brigitta*

1: Denial	19
2: Curiosity aroused	35
3: Meeting my other mother	43
4: Pandora's box	53
5: The final piece	65

PART 2: *Jo*

6: Are you my mother?	87
7: The search for self	107
8: Reunion reality bites	115
9: The after-effects	121
10: Waking up	129

PART 3: *Severed Ties*

11: I wanted you to have a family — Jan	151
12: The family that never was — Sue and Tony	163

PART 4: *The Legacy*

13: The ripple effect	173
Afterword	223
Appendices	227
Further reading	232
Acknowledgements	235
About the authors	237

Foreword

I first met Jo Willis at a Wellington conference on adoption and healing in 1997. She came with three other women who, like her — and like me — were adopted by 'strangers' during the era of closed adoption, and had all subsequently made contact with their birth families. As she explains in this book, they had come together over two years to make sense of their lives in relation to adoption. 'Despite remarkably diverse backgrounds, adoption experiences, lifestyles and personal circumstances … we shared the same core issues. The relief at being able to talk openly about adoption in a supportive environment was immense.'

As they generously shared their discoveries, I sat at the back of the packed room with tears pouring down my face. It was the first time I had heard anyone talk about these deeply embedded issues, especially the recurrent feelings of struggling with relationships and never quite belonging anywhere.

These were vitally important insights which needed to be widely shared. So I was immensely pleased to discover Jo's and Brigitta's book online, and learn that Massey University Press was publishing a revised and extended print edition.

The contrasting adoption and reunion stories that Brigitta and Jo tell here are uniquely accompanied by the perspectives of birthparents, partners and children, as well as their own insightful commentaries. Not only intensely moving, they also achieve precisely what the authors aimed for: 'To illuminate the complexity, the emotional challenges and the legacy of adoption', especially along the path of reunion, both for adopted people and for their 'partners, parents, children, siblings, friends and extended whānau'.

Their book demonstrates so effectively that no matter how difficult it can be, 'an awareness of the range of emotions being felt and a willingness to keep communicating and making decisions together can mean positive, long-term outcomes for all parties involved — even when initially there may be a strong temptation to pull back'.

Finally, and crucially: 'Although the relationships we have with others are critical, it is the relationship we end up having with ourselves that is most important … It is not just about surviving; it is about thriving with the new self who has emerged.'

Anne Else
February 2022

Prologue

I stepped out the back door of the house and hovered indecisively in the courtyard.

I could hear my husband speaking as he came down the steps not far from where I stood. He was answered by a cheerful sounding female voice.

'God, that's her,' I thought as waves of pure adrenaline flooded through me and my stomach began to churn. The realisation flashed through my mind that she sounded quite chatty and relaxed, then a stranger stepped into the courtyard and started walking towards me.

What should I do? Should I hug her? Was she a 'hugging' sort of person? What was even appropriate behaviour in this bizarre situation? What should I say?

Before I could summon reason, I was in her arms, crying like a lost child and never wanting to let go. For several minutes a spell held us bound as we rocked gently together. It felt perfectly natural. There was no hesitation from her, no holding back, no stiffness. I have no idea what she said to me until she gently took hold of my shoulders and whispered, 'Let me look at you properly.'

Introduction

> When we tell our stories, we change the world. We'll never know how our stories might change someone's life — our children's, our friends', our parents', our partner's or maybe that of a stranger who hears our story down the line or reads it in a book.
>
> — Brené Brown, *The Gifts of Imperfection*

For many adopted people, there is an almost insatiable hunger associated with not knowing who we are or where we came from. It is this hunger that drives many of us to search for our roots, to find the missing part of us, in the hope of finally having our questions answered. Being adopted does not make us unique in terms of the emotional challenges that affect our lives. Everyone has issues and limiting beliefs that affect the choices they make and the way they interact with others. Everyone has a story — adoption is just one. What is uniquely challenging about adoption is that, for those of us raised in the closed adoption era, it is almost the first experience in life; it defines us from the earliest hours of our existence.

Unfortunately, setting out to find the answers to the questions can be terrifying. The idea of taking the first step towards contact with a birthparent is often overwhelming, and the lifelong fear of not being wanted, of not being welcomed with open and loving arms, forces many of us to hesitate, to delay, to procrastinate. The excuses are endless: What if my birthmother isn't interested? Perhaps I was just a mistake that everyone wants to forget? How will I cope if a phone gets slammed down on me? What if I contact the wrong person and make an idiot of myself?

Then there is the question that overrides all others: What will I find? This fear of the unknown, of uncovering some unpleasant truth that will make us wish we had left well alone, can be an insurmountable hurdle for many.

And behind this question lies another — one that often goes unrecognised and unacknowledged. What are we actually looking for? Although the answer usually lies buried deep within our consciousness, many of us are looking for that safe haven, that loving connection that makes us feel unconditionally loved, secure and whole. A connection that allows us to be our true self and not feel rejected. A place where the grief and the sense of loss we have carried in our heart can be healed.

We are searching for the sanctity of our mother's arms.

•

Our aim in writing this book is to wake adopted people up to the impact adoption may have had on them, and to raise awareness and understanding about a topic that affects so many New Zealanders. It is the book we wish we had been able to read before setting out on our own paths to reunion — a hand to hold through the process. At times it was extremely difficult to write. It forced us to confront truths and reveal details that ran the risk of hurting some of those closest to us. But it was also very healing. Our intention is not to cause pain, but rather to illuminate the complexity, the emotional challenges and the legacy of adoption for adopted people as we write our own stories

The book is in four parts. We begin with our own journeys from adoption to reunion with our respective birth families, to the post-reunion experiences. The third and fourth are a series of other perspectives: our birthmothers, one birthfather, as well as our partners, and all four of our children, giving more insight into the impact of the reunion journey on those whom are closest to us.

Our two stories provide a real contrast in experiences, not only in the adoption process and growing up as adopted children but also with our birth families following the reunion. One of us made a choice to wait many years before pursuing reunion, which meant a degree of maturity and fewer expectations but then dealing with grief over having missed out on a birthmother's presence for so long. For the other, the first meeting with our birthmother came at age 21, which triggered another painful experience of rejection that made it difficult to have trust in the relationship going forward.

For adopted people, understanding how we may have been impacted by relinquishment is key to recognising potential triggers and self-limiting beliefs when it comes to our wider interpersonal relationships. Helping the people we are closest to understand why we sometimes behave the way we do, and accepting that we can't simply 'get over it' and may need extra support, can have a big impact on our emotional wellbeing. Having people in our life who validate our experiences and accept us for who we are is extremely important.

We sincerely hope that as well as helping other adopted people feel they are not alone in their experience, our stories may enlighten other affected partners, parents, children, siblings, friends and extended whānau. If we can shine a light on what has traditionally been hidden around adoption and its legacy, then perhaps those of us who have experienced adoption first-hand may find greater understanding and empathy for the challenges we face.

What we have found through our own experiences of adoption and reunion is that, although the relationships we have with others are critical, it is the relationship we end up having with *ourselves* that is most important. Finding peace of mind, feeling genuinely happy and okay about who we are, and being authentic in how we live our life — despite the early trauma of separation from our birthmother — is what really counts. It is not just about surviving; it is about thriving with the new self who has emerged.

No matter which side of the adoption equation you are on, the journey will almost always be tinged with a degree of sadness. You can't undertake it without having to confront the 'what might have been' questions and recriminations. Adopted people and birth families at some point often have to accept that some of the things they missed out on can never be reclaimed.

We know from personal experience how healing it can be when others articulate the raw emotions we ourselves are experiencing, and we truly hope that people who read our stories will not only appreciate our honesty but also will find healing through our words.

Despite the emotional turmoil, for us the journey has been worth taking.

Above: Me aged eight months; on a kindergarten float in Gore, aged four.
Below: With my two brothers, aged five.

PART 1

Brigitta

CHAPTER 1

Denial

> I wonder if I've been changed in the night?
> Let me think. Was I the same when I got up this
> morning? I almost think I can remember feeling
> a little different. But if I'm not the same, the
> next question is, who in the world am I?
>
> — Lewis Carroll, *Alice's Adventures in Wonderland*

My adoptive parents were living in Gore, a small town at the bottom of the South Island, when I was born in 1968. They already had two sons but wanted a daughter to 'round out' the family, and because my adoptive mother hadn't had an easy time with her pregnancies, they didn't want to risk another attempt. They'd actually been offered another child before me — a baby girl — but she didn't look enough like my brothers to 'fit' into the family. It sounded like shopping for a pair of shoes. It was one of the first stories I remember hearing about my adoption, about how they'd passed over this other child because they felt it was important that the hair colour was the same, the eyes were similar to my brothers', and that the child 'matched'. I used to wonder what happened to her.

The other story I often heard was that when they collected me, I was brought into the room in a well-worn Salvation Army gown, one that no doubt had been used by dozens of adopted babies. My adoptive mother was a wonderful dressmaker and had sewn a lovely little outfit for me, probably smocked and beautifully embroidered, and my two brothers, who were pre-schoolers at the time, insisted that my mother change me there and then into this new outfit so that I was 'turned into' their sister as soon as possible. Alarmingly, my brothers then held me for two hours in the back seat of the car as we drove to Gore. There were no car seats, of course. I think the boys even gave me my first bottle.

My early impressions, therefore, were of being chosen over someone else, the specialness of the new clothing, and my brothers being really enthusiastic. The whole family was on board; I was the treasured daughter, and now the family was complete. In some ways it gave me a sense of entitlement and belonging — the opposite experience to many adopted people who speak of not fitting in or feeling like an alien in their family.

·

From the outside, my childhood probably looked quite idyllic and, for the most part, it was. We lived on the edge of town, surrounded by paddocks where we were free to roam. We played with the neighbourhood kids, went to the local school, and although my parents were not well off, we had everything we needed. It was a typical country childhood and I didn't feel that being adopted set me apart in any way. I don't remember being told I was adopted; it was just always there. I don't have any recollection of realising that Mum and Dad were not my 'real' parents.

We had a book called *Mr Fairweather and His Family*, which was about a man who lived alone and how he came to have a family with a wife, a cat, a dog and, eventually, two adopted children. It was probably the standard text handed out to families like ours and I had some vague idea that the book related to my situation, but I wasn't really sure how. I don't think I felt any personal connection with the story; it was just another book among the many at my disposal. I was an avid reader and loved to go outside and sit under the trees in our large garden to read.

I don't remember asking my parents many questions about being adopted, and I didn't have any conscious thoughts around the word itself. When I went to the small local primary school, there were actually four of us who were adopted in my class alone. We weren't considered anything special, and I remember thinking it was no big deal. Neither do I have memories of fantasising about my birthmother or dreaming of finding her. I've read a lot of stories about adopted people who had these sorts of dreams, but I certainly never thought about her. There wasn't a lot of space for curiosity regarding my birth family and origins — my parents never talked about it when I was young, so I followed their lead and didn't raise the subject.

Reflecting on it now, I probably did feel quite secure. There was a strong sense of being a core part of the family, and possibly that was to do with it being a very small family. Both my parents were raised as only children (my father's four siblings all died as infants in pre-war England), so there were only the five of us — no aunts, uncles, cousins, and only one grandmother in New Zealand. There was a realisation that other people had extended families and we didn't, but my parents would say how lucky we were that we didn't have to put up with difficult relatives at Christmas. They made it seem like a good thing.

My brothers didn't look alike, even though they were related by blood, and I would often point out to people the similarities *I* had with my adoptive parents, such as having curly hair and being tall like my dad. I looked for things that were the same, and being part of a small family meant I didn't have a lot of mirroring back of characteristics I was lacking that were shared by a wider family group. The beliefs of the time were very much oriented towards nurture over nature as the greater influence. It was only as an adult that I allowed myself to realise how very different I was from the rest of my adoptive family.

Our only extended family was my grandmother. She remarried when I was five, but from when I was about nine, she and my step-grandfather were estranged from my parents, and I didn't see them for a number of years. My mum would talk about what a bleak childhood she had endured due to Nana's cold and unaffectionate mothering style. I found out many years later that Nana hadn't wanted my parents to adopt me, and had always preferred the boys, apparently bringing them presents and 'forgetting' one for me when I was little. I never had any sense of that; I just thought she didn't like girls, rather than her disapproving of me specifically.

I was the chatterbox in the family, once bending my father's ear to such an extent when he was driving that he crashed into another car while turning around to tell me to stop talking! My father's job was a big part of our lives. He was an electrical engineer and looked after all the mechanical equipment on the racecourses in Southland. He had a lot of staff, and some of those people became like extended family to me. We pretty much grew up on racecourses, and we all had jobs to do from quite a young age.

Dad was the boss at work, and I have strong memories of him being adored by the women who worked for him. He called everyone 'sweetheart' and 'love'. It was quite a social environment; he really looked after his staff, and there'd be drinks put on at the end of race day. He was well respected, and that same desire for respect has been a huge theme for me. Dad was larger than life. His was a strong personality and he ruled the roost, so my early impressions of family life were all about him. I felt like I shone when I was in his presence.

Dad was an intelligent man and could easily have gone to university, but he was from a working-class background and it wasn't encouraged. Instead, he was sent to war at 18, serving in the Middle East as part of the Royal Engineers in the British Army, so it was vitally important to him that all three of us kids received a tertiary education.

Under the surface of what appeared to be an ordinary family, things were not as stable as they seemed. My mother struggled with depression and was later diagnosed with bipolar disorder. She had a breakdown when I was about eight months old, and I went away to a facility in Dunedin with her.

She apparently also had breakdowns after the births of both boys. As an adult, I find it incredible that despite her history of instability, the authorities of the time didn't seem to question her suitability as an adoptive parent. Years later, when I worked up the courage to ask her about this period, she told me in a matter of fact way that when she was in the 'hospital' (psychiatric institution), she used to hand me over to another patient, a man who she'd become friendly with, while she went and had her 'sessions'. She said she didn't think she ever had shock treatments, but this man did after he'd finished his stints of babysitting me! I tried to be casual while asking her what impact this might have had on me, being handed over to a random stranger in such circumstances, but she responded quite indignantly, saying, 'It was really good therapy for him to look after you — he adored you!'

Throughout the first eight years of my life, there were other periods when my mother was very unwell and would detach from all of us. She would take to her bed for days at a time, and I remember feeling scared when she did that. I didn't really understand what was wrong; I just thought she had the flu or something similar. I actually have no memories of her being emotionally present when I was young. Because of the way she was raised and her inability to reach out, I don't remember her cuddling me or showing me affection. I had no conscious feeling that there was anything odd about that, but when I was older, she did explain that, because of not being hugged as a child herself, she felt stiff and awkward with physical closeness.

One time, when I was about seven, I crashed my brother's bike on the gravel road we lived on. My forehead was all cut up and grazed. Dad popped me into bed with Mum — she must have been having one of her episodes — and she didn't say anything to me, she didn't ask if I was okay, she didn't hold or comfort me, she just looked through me as if I wasn't there. I must have been a bit of a mess, because I've still got the scars from the accident, but she just lay there. Even now, as a parent and with a greater understanding of mental health issues, I look back on this and wonder about her lack of response. She must have been extremely unwell.

When she retreated to her bed, Dad used to take over. He was the affectionate one, the one who always cuddled and held me, and so in some ways, I feel that he buffered me from what I missed out on with Mum. Dad filled the space when she was emotionally absent. He protected me, made me feel special and gave me a degree of resilience. When I was eight, another breakdown took her away to a residential facility for a while, although I don't remember how long for and I don't recall missing her particularly. But I do remember a sense of shame associated with that time and being terrified that kids at school would find out where she was.

When she came home from hospital, she appeared to let go of a lot of things that used to worry her; she was more relaxed and positive. She decided to train as a social worker when I was in my early teens. It was something she chose to go and do that was separate from anyone else in the family, and I remember those years as being happy for her. She gained confidence and felt she'd found something she really loved. We probably had the closest relationship during that time. I had lots of freedom, but she was there if I needed her. There were certainly no more episodes of her taking to her bed.

But, unfortunately, by the time she was well again we had lost the chance to establish the bond that would normally have formed when I was a baby. Her mental health issues had prevented the vital emotional connection between mother and child from developing; a connection that had been harder to establish in the first place, given I'd been separated from my first mother as a newborn. Years later, I came to realise that it was this lack of healthy attachment to a mother, along with my relinquishment as a baby, that significantly impacted my ability to connect with women and to trust female relationships. I believe it also forced me to become emotionally independent from a young age, and to avoid situations where I felt vulnerable.

One of the other defining moments in my childhood that impacted my sense of security as an adopted child resulted from an interaction with my eldest brother. When I was about six years old and Nana was staying with us, my brother and I had some sort of disagreement. Things were always tense in the house when my grandparents visited, as they were big drinkers and smokers, plus my grandmother was very demanding and treated my mother like a servant at times. On this occasion,

I remember Nana and Mum being in the room and my brother getting annoyed with me over something minor and saying to me, 'Well, you're not really my sister anyway.'

It was a tiny comment, but at the time it felt huge. Everything I had known and believed about myself seemed to rush out the window. I felt like I had been punched in the stomach. My brother had no idea how much it hurt, but what went through my mind was, 'He's right, I'm not really his sister, and maybe I don't belong.' The fact that neither of the adults in the room reprimanded him or made any sort of comment only reinforced to me that it must be true.

As irrational as it sounds, I don't think I ever forgave him for it. Up until then he had been my adored older brother, but now I believed I knew how he really felt about me, and it was the first time I remember feeling unloved and unwanted. It was horrible. I've always been very black and white about people, something that has caused problems in my relationships; you're either on my side or you're out. Completely out. From that point on, he was out, and I spent the rest of my childhood alternating between trying to win his approval and tormenting him to the point where he couldn't stand me. Any brother–sister bond I'd believed in was broken with that one comment.

I had probably formed a strong attachment to him as a parental figure, given my mother's absences, and my other brother was a quiet, highly sensitive kid, so my eldest brother was the boss and we both looked up to him. Even when I was a teenager, his approval still meant so much to me, although I'm sure he was unaware of it. When I became dux of my high school, he was away at university, and I remember Mum making me speak to him on the phone so he could congratulate me. All he said to me was, 'Yeah, you made dux, but it's only in the arts subjects.' That comment is more clearly remembered than all the people who said, 'Well done, you worked hard for it, good on you.'

●

As a child you can't rationalise other people's behaviour. You don't understand that they have their own reasons for acting in certain ways; all you can do is deal with your own reaction to it. The way I coped was to prove that I was better than anyone else. My whole life became geared towards beating people, whether that be academically, professionally, or in the amount of attention I received. Being the 'perfect performing daughter' was the role I played out within my family; I felt I had to keep it up in order to be accepted, and because my father, especially, expected a lot of me. I saw his disappointment when my brothers did things he didn't like, and I didn't ever want him to look at me and think I was anything less than perfect. I didn't feel I could be loved just for myself — I needed to be successful, to achieve and make him proud. This was pressure I put on myself, but the need for external affirmation from my father set a pattern for the rest of my life.

My strong internal drive to keep proving my worth mainly applied to things I knew I could excel at. I was never any good at team sports, so I just didn't compete. My adoptive parents weren't really sporty, so I was never particularly encouraged in anything sports-related except swimming, which I was very good at. I remember being thrilled when my swim coach suggested to my parents that I take up competitive training, but my father felt it would impact negatively on my schoolwork, so I dropped the idea. He said it was my decision, but I was so desperate for his approval, there was no way I would go against what he wanted.

Our family was musical, particularly my mother, so she really encouraged this in all of us. I loved ballet and any form of dance, but as soon as I was old enough to learn an instrument, I gave up ballet and trotted off after my brothers to music lessons, because that's what was expected. I started with recorder, then clarinet, then flute, and I learnt piano when I went to high school, as well as musical theory. However, it was schoolwork where I really excelled, and because I knew how important academic success was to my father, I pushed myself hard.

·

As I matured, adoption became less of a taboo subject. My sense was that my mother was willing to talk about it, but I didn't really want to raise it in front of my father. I think her social work gave her more awareness of what was happening in the adoption field in terms of legislative changes, and she used to talk about having contact with Jigsaw, an organisation that helped connect adopted people with their birthparents. But despite her occasional prompts, I rarely expressed any interest in knowing more. I think I didn't want to do anything to spoil Dad's image of me as his daughter; I wanted the fantasy to continue.

The subject of adoption would usually come up over my name, which my parents spelt 'Briggita'. It was pronounced with a hard 'g'; a Germanic pronunciation, which with my father's Scandinavian roots was a version he would have found familiar. When people asked where it came from, there would be this pause. My parents would never say straight out that I was adopted and the name came with me, but it always felt a little tense and they would be vague about it. I knew that being adopted meant I had this weird name, but I quite liked that it was different. My thoughts never went any further than that. I didn't think about the person who had chosen it. I didn't think about the existence of another mother who gave me up.

When I was about 16 years old, my adoptive mother gave me a small white Bible that my birthmother had left for me. It wasn't linked to my birthday or any particular event; I just walked into her bedroom one day and she handed it over, saying something like, 'I thought it was about time I gave you this.' I was shocked, but still my main thought in that moment was, how does she want me to react? I was looking to her for the cue to how to respond, rather than feeling anything for myself. But I do remember wanting to know more. Perhaps she realised this, because she told me that my parents weren't young teenagers, they were a couple, but they were not ready to have a baby. I think she was trying to let me know they were 'legitimate' in some way.

Interestingly, she didn't give me the Bible when Dad was around — it was something private between the two of us.

I'm not sure she even told him about it, and it was certainly never discussed in front of him. Years later, after I met Jan, my birthmother, and we talked about the Bible, Dad said he remembered one of the staff members at the Salvation Army home shaking it first to make sure there were no hidden notes inside before handing it over. He could still recall, after 40 years, how careful they were that nothing was passed on from my birthmother.

Receiving the Bible didn't cause any real shift in my awareness, even though it was the first physical evidence that it was true, that I was adopted, and there was another mother who had left me this gift. There was a photo of me inside it, taken when I was 10 days old — the day I would have been handed over — and I remember having a reaction to that. I looked really ugly and I thought, no wonder she gave me up if I looked like that! But I carried the Bible as I walked down the aisle on my wedding day, and although I hadn't begun to look for my birthmother at that stage, on some level I think I wanted her to be part of the occasion.

·

I never really rebelled as a teenager, but there was a lot that I kept hidden from my parents. Nothing that would particularly shock them, but I had a strong sense that I didn't really need people and enjoyed being independent, so I just didn't confide a lot about what was going on for me.

I kept quite an emotional distance from most people, the one exception being my best friend, Justine, who lived next door. She went to a different school, but we spent almost every weekend together. As close as we were, however, I never talked to her about adoption, and she never shared with me how volatile her home life was. When her parents spilt up, I remember being completely shocked that she hadn't disclosed to me how rough things were at home. Perhaps as teenagers we just didn't know how to share our inner worlds.

Being adopted wasn't something I kept a secret growing up. There was no shame; I just preferred to keep up the illusion that I was part of an intact family. When people found out, they would say things like, 'Oh, you're adopted; you don't look it.' I was never quite sure how I was supposed to respond when I heard that. Then the next question would be: 'Have you ever thought about finding your birthmother?' I remember whenever this question was asked of me in front of my parents, my response was always 'I'm not that interested' or 'I don't feel I need to look for her'. The reaction was provoked by wanting to do what I thought would please them.

There was a lot of bravado from me about adoption not affecting me. I grew up in this fantasy world, convincing myself that I really was the 'natural' child of my adopted parents, and repressing any thoughts or feelings associated with my birthmother. As for my birthfather, I never even considered him. I lived my life accepting that the slate had been wiped clean when I was handed to my new parents. My childhood and teenage years were characterised by a complete denial that adoption had had an impact on my life.

I didn't ever make a judgement about my birthmother and I never felt any blame towards her, I just didn't want my adoptive parents to feel that I wasn't grateful they had taken me in. I felt that admitting to curiosity about my origins would somehow be a betrayal.

I kidded myself for nearly 40 years that adoption hadn't had an impact on me, but when I started examining it and looking at the patterns, I could see adoption issues playing out. The key themes were craving acceptance through approval-seeking behaviour and hating being seen as vulnerable. I saw my adoptive mother as someone who was vulnerable, and the last thing I wanted to do was to be like that because, to me, it was a sign of weakness. I wanted to be seen in my father's mould — strong. I had to be strong and capable to be okay. Perhaps at some deeper level it was why I never allowed myself to yearn for my birthmother; that would have allowed vulnerability in.

Having heard so many stories of the pain that many adopted children go through during childhood and early adolescence, I can see that, despite my own childhood not being perfect, I did escape relatively unscathed. I have to give my adoptive parents credit for that. They didn't have all the skills needed to support me in accepting myself for who I was, but they thought they were doing the right thing, and it was the best that they could give with the information they had available to them at the time.

But as I became an adult, life's challenges started to create cracks in the persona I was presenting to the world.

CHAPTER 2

Curiosity aroused

> I don't feel I have the right — that's one of the pathological complications of adoption — that adoptees don't really have rights. Their lives are about supporting the secrets, the needs, and the desires of others.
>
> — A. M. Homes, *The Mistress's Daughter*

I had done well at university, gaining a first-class honour's degree in history and sociology at Canterbury University. I travelled extensively, and then worked in London for several years. On my return to New Zealand, I reconnected with the love of my life, Andrew (whom I had actually met on my first day at university), and we married and moved to Sydney, where we both worked for large multinational companies, me in recruitment and HR consulting. I was in control of my life and everything was going according to plan.

We both wanted a family and within a year of marriage, our daughter was born. I felt very blessed — but motherhood opened up a deep core of emotional turmoil I had kept buried for over 30 years. Suddenly I didn't feel so capable anymore; in fact, my life felt completely out of control. I was overwhelmed by the demands of this tiny creature in my care, and it was as if I were living someone else's life. At first I presumed my feelings were a normal reaction to adjusting to the dramatic changes brought about by new motherhood, but as the years went by, and our second daughter was born, I still couldn't find a way to feel satisfied with my life. Something was missing.

We moved back to New Zealand and I tried everything I could to get happy. I started studying again, undertook volunteer work, saw several counsellors, and eventually returned to paid employment. I had hoped that taking on another challenging role would give me back my sense of self-worth, but I was miserable. I had fallen into my old habits of seeking external validation and approval from others rather than looking within. This time, the familiar strategy didn't work.

I was also struggling to connect with my eldest daughter and believed there were deeply buried feelings of anger and discontent that tainted some of my interactions with her. My marriage was suffering, and I was worried that my children were going to miss out in some way because I was a hopeless mother. I remember saying to a therapist around this time that my children were fantastic kids despite my mothering, not because of it. The look of shock that briefly passed over his face made me realise just how flawed my thinking had become. Slowly through the sessions I became aware that many of my issues tied back to motherhood. Although we briefly explored my experience of adoption, I was still in denial that being adopted had affected me in any way.

It wasn't until I worked with a life coach that I was pushed to explain why I had never searched for my birthmother. My coach was a wise and mature woman who pointed out to me that not knowing my birthmother may be having an impact on my ability to mother my own daughters. I remember the jolt of realisation that went through my body as I thought, I could actually try to find her. Having someone challenge me on it and to know that I had run out of excuses was a turning point.

It seems inexplicable that I lacked curiosity about my background for so long. I had never fantasised about who this 'alternative' mother could be and I didn't think I was yearning for something that was missing. I always believed the mother–daughter bond I shared with my adoptive mother was 'good enough' and that I had no needs beyond this. During my late teens and twenties, when people found out I was adopted, the same questions would come up: 'Have you found your birthmother?'; 'Are you curious about her?'. Still, there would be no picture of her in my mind, no sense of wanting to know anything about who she was or what she was like. I never imagined anyone who looked like me, was tall like me, had olive skin like me.

Having my children changed all that, particularly since my eldest daughter was the spitting image of me when I was a child. Motherhood forced me to confront the fact that I had no genetic or medical knowledge about my background. When I was pregnant and had been required to answer questions about my background and fill out forms, I could only leave them blank. Not knowing anything about my birthmother's experience of pregnancy or whether she'd had any medical issues suddenly mattered.

So, the idea that it would be good to know, at some point, was certainly planted during pregnancy, but it took several more years for me to do something about it. Examining my feelings about my adoption was a foreign concept to me. I quickly swapped any acknowledgement of my own agenda for the more 'worthy' cause that I was just trying to allay any fears *she* might have about what happened to me. I genuinely believed that my only motivation was to be able to tell her she had done the right thing in giving me up.

•

The first step was to apply for my original birth certificate from the Registrar General's office. I received a letter telling me that the Department of Child, Youth and Family Services, the government department that managed all adoption records at that time, would contact me. Simple enough, except the certificate I received in the mail a few weeks later was a copy of the post-adoption one I already had. Here was the first hurdle and I'd stumbled. I thought, maybe this is a sign that I'm not supposed to find her?

For nine months I did nothing further, rationalising that I hadn't been particularly motivated in the first place. Then one day I woke up and thought, this is crazy, I'm being a wimp! My thirty-ninth birthday was fast approaching, and I decided that if I was going to make contact with my birthmother, I wanted to do it before I turned 40.

I re-applied for my original birth certificate explaining that I had been sent the wrong one and within days a letter arrived. It was a Monday morning. I opened the envelope with a mixture of dread and excitement. I was stunned to see how much information it contained; my post-adoption certificate had only been a third of the size. The first thing that struck me was that my name was spelt incorrectly. I knew my adoptive parents had kept the name I had been given at birth, but for all these years, it had been spelt with two 'g's and one 't', yet here it was in black and white, spelt the other way around, *Brigitta*. For now, I parked the issue about my name, knowing I would revisit it. But quietly, I would sometimes find myself rolling the softness of the consonants around in my head, *Brigitta*, like a sigh of wind, and I realised how long I had been dealing with a name that I found difficult to manage and had subsequently preferred to use the shortened version of 'Brigs'.

More importantly than my name, however, was my birthmother's name: Janice Katherine Harvey. It was real; I did have another mother. Enclosed with the birth certificate was a pamphlet that explained how to go about searching, and information about the availability of a support person to assist with the process, but I was too impatient for that. Now that I'd taken the first step, I didn't want to pause and be sensible.

My husband urged me to keep going. I left the children with him and headed into the central library in Auckland. I knew marriage certificates and electoral rolls might help, so I asked for assistance from one of the librarians. I felt self-conscious actually admitting what I was up to, but he was very helpful and confirmed that the best place to start was to find out if my birthmother had married. If she had, knowing her married name would be crucial to finding her. The details of all New Zealand marriage certificates were held on microfiche. I remember thinking how incredibly old fashioned this was and wondering whether I'd still know how to use the machine, then as soon as I saw so many banks of files, my heart sank. How would I ever find what I needed? But there was only one thing to do and that was to start looking. I decided I would give myself a ten-year period from my birth date. I figured if my birthmother hadn't married within that timeframe, I'd have to come up with a new plan. For all I knew she could have left the country, got divorced or even died.

I slid microfiche files into the machine and scanned for the surname 'Harvey'. It was a common name, and yet for the decade of records I diligently searched through, I didn't find a single 'J. Harvey'. In the very last year of files, just when I was ready to give up, I came across a 'J. K. Harvey' beside the name 'C. Parker', and a date — that was all. There was no further information about where the marriage had taken place or the full names of the couple. Surely this couldn't be her?

I jotted down the details, then started flicking through the electoral rolls, but it seemed pointless. 'Parker' was even more common than 'Harvey' and I had no idea where she might have been living. My birth certificate had stated her birthplace as Masterton, but she probably hadn't stayed there. Strangely, it was the same town my husband had grown up in, but when I phoned him to ask if he knew anyone around her age with either surname, he drew a blank. I had already been at the library for several hours; it was time to admit defeat and go home.

I felt very confused by what I had experienced that day. I honestly hadn't thought I was terribly motivated to find my birthmother, but now that I had touched her life by seeing her name on my birth certificate, I felt driven to know more. I went home feeling deflated and called Andrew again to tell him I was at a dead end. He wasn't so ready to give up. As soon as I walked in the door, he beckoned me over to the computer and told me we might be able to find an address through the online telephone directories. 'It's not going to be that easy,' I replied, 'I don't even know if the marriage details I found are hers, and there must be hundreds of Parkers in New Zealand.'

He wouldn't be put off, though, and our search turned up just one couple that matched the initials we were looking for.

'It's not them,' I said. 'We're looking for a needle in a haystack.'

'Call the number anyway,' he said.

'No bloody way, you call it!'

'All right, I will.'

Suddenly a surge of panic overtook me. This couldn't be happening so fast. I made him go into the spare bedroom — I just couldn't bear to watch him make the call. What would he say? How would he explain who he was? Surely, we'd got the wrong person and it would all be horribly embarrassing. No way could it be this easy to find a missing person. Realistically I was probably facing months of dead ends. Why was he taking so long?

Finally, the bedroom door opened. He came out looking shocked and pale. He said two words.

'It's her.'

CHAPTER 3

Meeting my other mother

> That word — genetic — had an almost sacred meaning to me. A genetic link, a magical bond. An inexpressible essence of belonging and being.
>
> — Nicky Campbell, *Blue-eyed Son*

The floor seemed to drop away in front of me. I can't even describe the feeling — it was a mixture of elation and terror. I didn't know how to deal with the speed of the news, or the confusion I felt.

Andrew told me that my birthmother had answered the phone with the words 'Jan speaking', and he was immediately thrown. Was this the Janice we were seeking or someone different? He told her he was looking for a Janice Katherine Harvey and she said, 'That would be me.' Nervously he then asked if the name 'Briggita' meant anything to her.

She hesitated as if she'd misheard, then said, 'It does.'

He explained that he was my husband, that I was adopted, and that we thought I might be her daughter. At that point she simply said, 'Yes, she is.'

He asked if she would like to speak to me. She paused and then said, 'If I don't speak to her now, I may never speak to her.'

Realising that he hadn't cleared this with me yet, he said, 'Shit, I don't know if she wants to talk to you!' They agreed that he would go and ask me and, whatever the outcome, one of us would call her back within the next 10 minutes.

As soon as he relayed this conversation to me, I knew I had to call her. Because I had convinced myself that my motivation for searching was to put to rest any fears or worries she had carried about me over the years, my whole focus was on her. I thought, she's a mother and I'm just going to tell her the things she wants to know. This thought got me over to the telephone and as I dialled the number, a strange calm came over me. I was doing this for her, not me. I knew her journey would have been much harder than mine. After one ring the voice of my other mother answered with an uncertain 'Hello.'

'Hi, it's Briggita,' I said. 'How are you?'

The conversation lasted for almost two hours. I don't even remember most of what we talked about. She shared some of her background and the story of meeting my birthfather. I told her exactly what I had wanted to say: that I had enjoyed a great life, had been raised by loving parents, and that she had done the right thing when she gave me up. She cried when I said those words and I could hear the relief in her voice. She told me her husband and family knew nothing about me and she had given up any hope of ever hearing from me.

We didn't make any specific plans, I simply told her at the end of the conversation that there was no pressure from me but I would like to stay in touch. I asked for her address so that I could send her some photos. She said she would write when she'd had a chance to process everything, but that it was difficult for her to speak on the phone because of her husband. He happened to be out that night, but she confessed if he'd been home, she might not have had the courage to speak to me. I wondered what this comment implied, but I was happy to do whatever she wanted and to take the next step at a pace she was comfortable with. I had read a little bit about how difficult reunion relationships could be, so I knew I didn't want to push her.

When I got off the phone, I felt completely drained, but a sense of calm remained. I had finally done the 'right' thing. I'd pushed myself to make contact and because it had all happened so quickly and with such ease, I felt the timing was exactly as it should be. Later would come the regrets — that I had left it so long, that I'd denied my birthmother the chance to know my children as babies, that I'd lost the opportunity to enjoy her mothering influence earlier in my life — but for that night I was at peace with the way things had unfolded. Andrew and I talked for hours after the call, dissecting every word she had said. We speculated about where things could go from here. I knew I wanted to meet her. I felt I was on an emotional escalator taking me ever upwards, and now I didn't want to get off.

I posted photos of the girls and myself to Jan. A letter arrived not long after. I could tell that it had been hard for her to express herself on paper as the writing was stilted at times, as if she was holding something back. The strongest message that came through was her gratitude that I had finally laid to rest all her years of worrying and wondering if she had done the right thing. At one point she wrote: *The first thing I want to say is 'thank you' for that phone call. So much of what we talked about is a blur, but the one thing I remember very clearly is that you answered the one question I have wanted to ask for nearly 40 years, 'Have you been happy and well cared for?' and you answered that so emphatically that it has completely put my mind at rest.*

She also talked about family likenesses that she had picked up from the photos. It felt surprisingly thrilling to know there were actually people in the world who looked like me, and that my eldest daughter in particular had inherited some family traits.

We wrote to each other for several months, but Jan was very careful to let me be the one to drive the relationship forward. We agreed to meet in the summer after we got back from a family Christmas in Australia. Although it was now more than four months since I had made contact with Jan, she still hadn't told her husband or anyone else about me, and so, logistically, we had to be quite careful when making the arrangements. Jan indicated that she and her husband both had things in their past that they didn't discuss, and I didn't want to upset the tentative link between us by asking too many questions before meeting her.

Eventually it was decided that we would come down to Napier, which was close to where Jan lived, and stay with

Andrew's aunt and uncle. Jan would meet us at their home. The girls would go out with Andrew's family for the morning, as we knew it would be an emotional meeting and the situation was far too confusing to explain to a four- and six-year-old. We also didn't know if we would see Jan again after this first meeting, so we didn't want to introduce her to our children if it was going to be a one-off event. I hadn't told my adoptive family what I was up to at that point, terrified they would be hurt that I had searched for my birthmother or not even understand why I was doing this. The old guilty feelings of appearing ungrateful for the life they had given me was a big part of why I kept this meeting to myself.

However, I did ask Andrew's mother to join us in Napier. I knew she would be supportive of Andrew and me, as well as possibly making things a little easier for Jan, seeing as they were about the same age and she had cared for birthmothers as a nurse during the period when Jan had given me up for adoption. She had also adopted a son during the closed adoption era, and worked as a counsellor, so she was skilled at handling situations where strong emotions were at play.

·

I will never forget the intensity of the feelings that overwhelmed me that weekend. I was hyped up and incredibly nervous, and I tried hard not to think about what scenarios could play out. I just stayed focused on the fact that I was doing this for Jan. I remember realising I had forgotten to pack shoes to match the outfit I had chosen to wear and absolutely panicking about not looking my best. Andrew's aunt rustled up something appropriate, but I was just a bundle of nerves as the clock ticked down to Jan's arrival time. I had spent a lifetime trying to control any situation I put myself into and here I was about to relinquish that steely grip and make myself truly vulnerable.

The house is on a steep hill in Napier with terrible parking access, so I made Andrew go up and wait on the street to make sure Jan could find a park. I paced up and down the hallway wondering what I should say when she appeared. When I couldn't stand being inside for another minute, I stepped out of the back door and stood on the concrete path. Suddenly I heard voices, and Jan came down the stairs from the street.

I walked towards her. A fleeting fear gripped me that this could be awkward, but then the next moment we were holding each other, and I was crying. Relief overwhelmed me. I was finally in the arms of my mother.

As we stood back from each other, she held me at arm's length and looked me up and down. Would she be disappointed in what she saw? To cover my nerves, I asked her something inane along the lines of 'Did you have trouble finding the house?' My throat tightened as more tears welled up and I realised I was incapable of holding a normal conversation. Luckily, Andrew was there to smooth things over and as he and Jan carried on chatting, I had my first opportunity to really study her.

My first thought was that she was quite short, quickly followed by the realisation that she looked shy. She seemed friendly and down-to-earth, dressed in a long denim skirt and smart white shirt. Her hair was silver, her face smooth. She was sturdily built, but so much shorter than me. I felt like a giant beside her. With a sinking feeling I realised that we looked nothing alike. I couldn't find a single feature I recognised as my own. I was still tongue-tied and at a loss for anything to say, but Andrew's mother, who was waiting in the living room, made Jan feel welcome and kept things on a social level as we came inside and got settled.

The next few hours passed in a blur. We certainly weren't short of things to talk about, but I felt quite overwhelmed at various points during the conversation. Andrew was as curious as I was and asked plenty of questions, although he was also very sensitive to the fact that there were things I needed to ask and he gave me the space to do this. There were lots of tears, particularly when Jan recounted the days spent in the nursing home before she had to hand me over. She said the Salvation Army home nurses couldn't have been kinder to her. Unlike many of the horror stories I had heard about these homes for 'unwed mothers' in the 1960s, Jan's story was one of support and understanding.

Listening to her account of the actual day my adoptive family collected me made me feel ill — in fact, the memory of that story still has the power to evoke a physical reaction of dread in my body. I simply cannot imagine the pain she must have experienced dressing me, feeding me for the last time, then mentally preparing herself for the moment of our parting. No matter how rational the decision made months before must have seemed, the physical and emotional separation from her newborn baby must have been almost unbearable.

Jan was incredibly open and honest with me right from our first meeting, particularly about her emotions surrounding my birth and adoption. It surprised me that a woman of her generation could share her innermost feelings to such an extent, even though on another level she seemed so practical and matter of fact.

She also shared some information about my birthfather, and struggled, it seemed, to keep a neutral tone about this person who had obviously hurt her deeply. She told us the story of how they had met and what had happened once she found out she was pregnant with me. Her strength and courage in dealing with her situation was astounding. At this point, I remember Andrew smiling at me as if to say, Now I know where your stubbornness and determination comes from.

After several hours of intense talking, we were all emotionally wrung out. Andrew and I decided that we wanted Jan to meet the girls, although she was very restrained and didn't push for this at all. It just felt right to introduce them, so Andrew called his uncle, and he brought the girls back to the house for lunch.

Jan was amazing. She must have been desperate to take those two blonde angels in her arms and hug them like only a grandmother could, but she didn't push herself forward in this way. The girls of course had no idea who she was, but Jan had such an ability to engage with children that they immediately warmed to her. She had told us that she'd trained and worked as a Karitane nurse after I was born, acknowledging that this had been a way to deal with the grief of not being able to mother me, and that she'd discovered a natural affinity with young children.

My throat choked watching Jan play on the floor with my girls that first day. It reiterated not only how much they had missed out on but also what I had been deprived of. I can't explain how I knew she would have been a wonderful mum; I just felt it. I ached to be the one down on the floor enjoying her undivided attention and accepting my rightful position at the centre of her world. I could see what a different experience of being mothered I could have had. The longing I experienced for this 'other' version felt truly devastating.

CHAPTER 4

Pandora's box

> Perhaps the biggest myth surrounding adoption reunion is that suddenly your life will be complete … often it has quite the opposite effect.
>
> — Julie Jarrell Bailey, *The Adoption Reunion Survival Guide*

When it came time for Jan to leave, we stood by her car and clung to each other. It had been all too quick, and although I'd had so many of my questions answered, I was desperate to spend more time getting to know her. We were both hesitant to express how much we wanted to stay in contact, but at some point during our goodbyes I said, 'I want this to be a beginning for us, not the end.' I saw the relief on Jan's face, then she said she would write again when she'd had a chance to think things through. I tried not to worry about the practicalities, given that Jan still hadn't told her husband about me, but somehow I knew she would become a part of my life.

After Jan left, I was buzzing. We spent the rest of the evening discussing what she had shared with us. We all liked her so much and I couldn't get over how easy she had been to talk to. When I mentioned how disappointed I was that we didn't look alike, Andrew said, 'Are you kidding? I could see so many similarities between you.' He insisted there were many things we had in common — the shape of our foreheads, the way we used our hands, certain personality traits. I was thrilled that he could tell we were mother and daughter.

The next day, as we were driving out of Napier, Jan called me on my mobile to tell me how much it had meant to her to meet me and be introduced to my family. I burst into tears after I got off the phone and we had to try to explain to the girls why I was upset. 'Mummy is just crying with happiness' didn't satisfy them. We hadn't felt the need to explain who Jan was when they had met her the day before, and so it was pretty tough for them to grasp the concept of a birthmother. We took the approach of simply answering their questions as honestly as we could. My eldest daughter struggled for a long time to make sense of why a mother would give a baby away, while the youngest, with the innocence of a pre-schooler, happily accepted the idea of Jan as her new Nanna. Jan was another person put on this planet to spoil her as far as she was concerned.

●

Jan was really the first person in my life, apart from Andrew, whom I'd opened up to, and I was able to almost from that first meeting. I felt I had nothing to lose. What was the point of pretending to be someone I wasn't anymore? Instinctively I knew that being honest about my feelings and my desire for a relationship with her was going to be the only way forward. I allowed myself to be vulnerable, to open myself up to hurt. Jan met me on equal terms with a level of emotional honesty I had rarely encountered in anyone before.

I'd been told in the past that I had a tough outer shell. Going into this reunion with Jan, I'm not sure how I managed to shed this shield. I'd had some therapy, which certainly helped, plus I had a bit of an understanding of the challenges of post-reunion relationships through my research. But feeling as if I didn't have any strong needs myself allowed me to let Jan have some needs. Jan later said she appreciated how non-judgemental I was, that I allowed her to tell her story and I gave her a degree of safety in the way I approached our meeting.

I returned to Auckland and we continued to write to each other. Jan's letters were full of love and warmth. There were regrets about what had happened in the past and the relationship she had missed out on with me, mixed with hope for a future where we could get to know each other.

I found myself wanting more and more from her. I couldn't stop thinking about her, she was always on my mind and I was desperate for the next contact, the next opportunity to connect. I felt I had to control my instinct to jump in the car and drive down to Hawke's Bay. I went from being fairly casual about the whole reunion process to a compulsion to find out as much as I could about my background and family history. Not being able to contact Jan by telephone or email was frustrating, but we couldn't risk Jan's husband answering if I called, and he controlled all the email correspondence. Writing and receiving letters was lovely, but it seemed a very slow way of getting to know each other. The idea of not being able to share something this personal with my husband was completely foreign to me — Andrew and I shared everything — so I had to keep reminding myself that every marriage is different, and Jan had to do this in her own time.

As the weeks went by, Jan found it harder and harder to keep her secret and finally, about a month after we met, she called to say she had worked up the courage to break the news to her husband, and it had gone very well. He had actually been relieved, as he had apparently been starting to worry that Jan was having an affair! It had been a very emotional experience for both of them, but now the door was open to further visits.

A few days later, I was shocked to receive a letter from him, telling me how wonderful he thought it was that I had tracked Jan down, and how sad he was that she hadn't told him earlier about me. Given that Jan and I had both been very apprehensive about how he would react to the news, I was thrilled that he appeared so accepting and was willing to share some very personal feelings with me. He wrote that he was looking forward to meeting me immensely.

Based on his response, we started making plans to visit them in the school holidays. Despite the letter, I was still anxious about meeting him in person. I expected he wouldn't be easy to win over, but I knew that I had to do my best to make a good impression if I wanted to have easy access to Jan in the future. From what she had told me he could be quite controlling and very protective of her, so I understood how important this first meeting would be.

Our first visit to Jan's home went well, although I was extremely nervous as we drove down. Their cosy farmhouse was warm and welcoming, filled with country touches that I loved. I noticed the copper pots and jelly moulds hanging on the kitchen wall, the wire basket on the bench filled with fresh eggs. It was comforting and homely. Even the bunches of spring flowers in vases in the bedrooms made me feel like we were being thought about and cared for. We had decided to spend only one night with them as we didn't want to push things, but by the next day, all of us were extremely reluctant to part company. The girls took to their new Poppa almost immediately, and he and Andrew established a strong bond. For me, however, there was definitely a degree of awkwardness between my stepfather and me during that first meeting, and unfortunately it never went away. I sensed that he saw me as some sort of threat to his relationship with Jan, that we were in competition for her affection. This attitude was to prove a stumbling block in the future.

On this visit we were also introduced to Jan's stepson and his two children, who were only a little older than my girls. Although I wasn't related to them by blood, we were immediately made to feel like family, my stepbrother even calling me 'sis' and embracing me with such warmth when we were introduced that I was overcome with a real sense of wellbeing. I knew how incredibly lucky I was to be welcomed in this way.

Now my remaining hurdle was to tell my adoptive parents about Jan. I put it off for weeks after we returned to Auckland.

They had been supportive of most major decisions I had made in my life, but we hadn't discussed the subject of my adoption for many years, and had certainly never talked about the idea of me searching for my birthmother. I feared they would be shocked and hurt to know that I had gone ahead and found her without telling them.

I reached a point where I simply had to get it over and done with. Jan was planning to visit us in Auckland and wanted to meet my parents, so Andrew and I eventually invited them over for dinner and I blurted it out over dessert. I tried hard to act nonchalant about the whole thing. Surprisingly, both my parents were incredibly positive — and even excited for me. Dad said that now I had found Jan, I had to keep her in my life because she had missed out on so much. I even discovered that they had known more about Jan and her circumstances than I had ever realised. It was such a relief to have told them and I was thrilled that they were so encouraging. Could this reunion experience get any better?

My fortieth birthday was looming. I had heard many accounts of adopted people describing how difficult birthdays were for them growing up, often because it was a reminder of their relinquishment, but I had always breezed through them. This changed after I met Jan.

On the morning of my birthday a huge bunch of beautiful flowers arrived from her. She also sent me a gold chain that had been passed down between four generations of eldest daughters in her family. I was the fifth. It was the first piece of family jewellery I'd ever owned, and I was overwhelmed. This acknowledgement that I really was part of her family and had my place in a genetic line felt incredibly precious, but it also triggered some very raw emotions. I felt I was back to being a small child, hurting for the loss of her mother and the loss of her birthright. I cried a lot on that day.

•

My interactions with Jan continued to be mostly positive and validating; however, my thoughts were tinged with sadness for the things I had missed out on. I was elated to hear from her and to spend time with her, but for several months after I got to know her, I felt I had to constantly push down feelings of grief and loss. Also, the reunion 'honeymoon' was over. As time went by, we developed a close mother–daughter bond, but it often felt like other people were intruding on our 'happily ever after'.

We had a lovely time hosting Jan and her husband when they visited us in Auckland yet, despite the affirming initial reaction from my parents towards the news of my reunion with Jan, the actual visit with them was difficult for me. My father greeted Jan with open arms and gave her a big hug when we arrived, but I could sense that Mum was intimidated and to some degree threatened by Jan. When they met, she only offered Jan her hand to shake. It seemed so formal and cold. I felt humiliated. This woman had given her the gift of a daughter for 40 years. In my head, I knew it must be hard for Mum, but in my heart, I was upset that she hadn't made more effort to make Jan feel welcome. In the end it was Jan who stepped forward and put her arms around my adoptive mother.

Afterwards, in the car going home, I burst into tears and sobbed while Jan held me. To me the visit had highlighted the differences between my two mothers: Jan allowed her natural feelings and instincts to be expressed; my adoptive mother held hers in check. It wasn't her fault that she was like that, but how I wished she'd been able to open up about her feelings and emotions. Jan had nothing but good things to say about both my parents, but I was still upset about what had happened.

This pattern of my adoptive mother being awkward and uncomfortable around Jan in my presence was to continue for years, although, interestingly, when it was just the two of them, Jan told me Mum was a lot more open and relaxed. Several months after meeting Jan, Mum did confess that although she considered Jan a friend, she felt some jealousy when she came into my life. This level of honesty was rare, though, and we didn't seem able to talk about my reunion easily. She would ask after Jan, but never enquire about how I was coping, what I was feeling, or how the relationship was progressing.

I felt I had to hold myself back regarding my feelings about Jan when I was with my adoptive parents. I felt guilty about my growing closeness to her and the ease with which we had slotted into each other's lives. For probably the first year after I met Jan, I wanted to distance myself from my adoptive family — somehow, they represented a false family history to me, and Jan and her extended family were a more authentic reflection of who I was as a person. When I was with my adoptive family, I felt cheated. I put pressure on myself to keep up the 'perfect performing daughter' role, but they would have been horrified if they had known what was going through my mind. It caused a lot of internal conflict for me when I spent time with them. My parents represented the tension between my historical role in my adoptive family and the flourishing that was taking place in my new relationship with Jan.

There was also an increasing tension in the relationship with my stepfather. He wasn't the sort of person to speak openly about his feelings, but his actions and attitude towards Jan demonstrated how insecure he felt about his relationship with her now that I was on the scene. I knew that he had alienated Jan from many of her family and friends over the years, and in the past she had gone along with his wishes. This time, she was prepared to stand up to him. But, as this dynamic in their relationship changed, I felt I was becoming the focus of his frustrations. He wasn't a bad person by any means and continued to be extremely generous to us, but he was used to having Jan all to himself. She made it very clear how important our relationship was to her, and he didn't like it.

Things weren't too bad when we were living in Auckland — Jan was 'allowed' to come and visit me on her own and we had regular contact, but after a wonderful summer holiday in Hawke's Bay, Andrew and I started talking about a possible move there. We had both fallen in love with the area, it was closer to Andrew's family, and our business allowed us the flexibility to live pretty much anywhere in New Zealand. We decided it would be a wonderful opportunity to get out of the Auckland rat-race and give our children the type of rural lifestyle we had both grown up with. The biggest attraction to me, of course, would be my proximity to Jan. I couldn't think of anything better than being physically close to her. There was a hunger to have her in my life and I wanted her to have a close bond with our daughters — while I was finding out more about myself through my connection with her. Quite simply, I wanted my mother around.

On the surface my stepfather seemed happy about our plans. However, once we moved, there were times when he seemed to be trying to restrict Jan's access to me. She and I talked a lot about the pressure this put on her. She felt conflicted by her desire to spend as much time as possible with us while recognising her husband's needs. It was a constant juggle. Because of the type of person she is, she wanted to keep everyone happy, but I found it hard not to show how frustrated I was with his controlling behaviour.

I knew it must have been difficult for him to have his peaceful, well-ordered life turned upside down by our arrival, but the petty childish side of me raged against his ability to spoil things for Jan and me. No matter how many times I said in my head, 'It's not about me, it's about his relationship with Jan', feelings of rejection would be triggered and I would overreact. I was also terrified that Jan would be forced to choose between us, and he had been in her life a lot longer than I had.

Fortunately, through all these challenges, Jan and I were able to keep talking honestly with each other. This was the key to getting through the rocky road of reunion. We made sure we met regularly without anyone else around. She would often say that if I felt the need to pull back, she would understand, and would always be there when I was ready to come back into her life. She knew better than anyone how difficult her husband could be, but she always reiterated how precious my family was to her. Honesty and clear communication between us during this period meant that there was less risk of misunderstandings.

●

One of the things I most enjoyed was the chance to meet Jan's wider family. I would have loved more opportunities to get to know them, but on the few occasions when we did have family gatherings, I was always made to feel incredibly welcome. Everyone was so happy for Jan that I had come back into her life. I remember my uncle's sixtieth birthday in Taupō. It was the first family celebration I was invited to, and at one point I looked around and thought, these are my people. It sounded corny even to my own ears, but that's what I felt. It was wonderful to be part of a large family group and to know I was one of them.

This feeling of belonging was, however, tinged with regret. The years of their Christmas, birthday and anniversary celebrations had created a bond that I would never share and a relationship of love that connected them. I was a stranger and I would never completely fit in because we didn't have a shared history. I would never know the grandparents they spoke of so fondly or get the family in-jokes that made up the rich fabric of their lives. It was great to suddenly have such a large, boisterous family, but I would always be an outsider. I could clearly see that I would have to do much of the work to feel included. As welcoming as they were, they didn't need me in their lives — I was the one longing to be accepted.

I also stood out because of my height — I towered over everyone else. Family members joked with me that my maternal side tended towards the short and stocky. They said I was lucky to have dodged that genetic bullet, but I still yearned for a physical likeness. Jan had told me the first time we met how like my birthfather I was — he was tall and of a similar build to me. He was the missing piece of the reunion puzzle.

CHAPTER 5

The final piece

Above all else we seek connection ... with the parts of ourselves we have repressed, with other people, and with the larger universe.

— Harville Hendrix, *Getting the Love You Want*

When I had started searching for Jan, the question of finding my birthfather had naturally been raised, but for me this wasn't a priority. My focus was on my birthmother. Then after I met Jan, I became a lot more curious about him, particularly given the strong reaction she'd had to my physical appearance when we first met. Even though she'd told me a little bit about him, I felt nervous asking for more information, knowing how much the thought of him upset her. She had blanked out almost everything about him from her memory, including his surname, so it would be difficult to trace him.

For at least a year after I found Jan, I did nothing more about my birthfather. I knew his first name was Bob and he was Australian, that he was about seven years older than Jan and had been working in South Africa. I also knew the name of the boat they met on — the *Northern Star* — and that he got off the boat in Sydney. That was about the extent of it. But the more I discovered about my origins, the more I wanted to find out. As the months went by, I found I wasn't content with only knowing one side of my story. Curiosity started eating away at me.

Yet what was I risking by going down this path of searching for Bob? Surely what I was developing with Jan should be enough? Could it destroy what I had with her? He had hurt her so badly and I knew the last thing she wanted was to have him back in her life or to bring up memories of the pain he had caused.

However, I couldn't blame Bob for what had happened. Despite how much I loved Jan and felt protective of her, Bob had his own story to tell and we didn't know why he had acted the way he did 40 years ago. Perhaps I had a right to know his reasons. I wondered if he might actually like to know that I existed. In reality, it was far more likely that he would want to leave the past in the past, but there was still a part of me that wanted to find out more.

The biggest barrier to me doing anything further to find Bob was the fact that Jan had lied to him and told him she'd had a miscarriage. I didn't know if I could confront a man now in his seventies with the shocking news that a child had in fact been born. Every birthmother, no matter what the circumstances of the conception and relinquishment of her child knows that they have carried a baby and given birth to it. Jan had thought about me for 40 years. She always knew at the back of her mind that there was a chance I would some day make contact. He had no idea. In the end, I convinced myself that there was no harm in trying to find out a little more about him. Whether I would have the courage or even the inclination to make contact was a bridge I could cross at a later date. Andrew pointed out to me that finding Jan had been an incredibly positive experience — why would it be any different with my birthfather?

I started by trying to find out more about the ship they'd met on. I knew the dates he was on board and where he got off, and again the internet was put to good use. I managed to find photos of the ship, plus some newspaper clippings about the actual voyage Jan and Bob had taken. There had been a fire on board when the ship had stopped in Durban, and the articles described the events (a story Jan had told me the first time we had met). There were some passenger lists available for various voyages during the 1960s, but I couldn't find any details about Bob. My efforts to dig up a surname through this avenue proved fruitless.

This was when I realised it was going to be impossible to get any further without Jan's help. But I was so worried about upsetting her and my desire to maintain our relationship was so strong, I decided to park Bob in the 'too hard' basket. It presented too much risk.

A turning point came about a year later when I decided to start writing about my experience of searching for my birthmother. I had been recording my feelings about the search for Jan and our reunion, with the idea of some day turning it into something I could share with others, but I wasn't really sure how to take it to the next level. In May 2011, I made contact with the Adoption Services Unit at the Department of Child, Youth and Family Services in Napier to try to find out if they held any records relating to my adoption. I mentioned to the woman who answered the phone that I was thinking about writing a book about my experiences as an adopted person. She jumped in excitedly and said that her boss, Jo Willis, had also spent years trying to write a book about adoption, and told me she would pass on my details.

A week later, Jo gave me a call and we set up a meeting. She and I clicked immediately. She was the first person I had met who encouraged me to speak openly and at length about my adoption. I was fascinated by her own story of reunion, and by the end of the conversation we agreed there was potential here for us to create something together. She had only recently made the decision that she wouldn't go any further with a book on her own. This is what I scribbled in my journal straight after the meeting:

> I've just come back from having a coffee with
> Jo. My hands were shaking as I got into the car
> afterwards. It was a real 'meeting of the minds' but
> so much more than that too — shared experiences,
> emotions, hurts and triumphs. She is the first

adopted person I have met who has really 'got' me. She is also so much further along in her journey than me — so strong, passionate, and articulate about the value she has gained from her experiences. By comparison I felt very fragile, broken, and stilted. But I also feel excited by the possibility that together we might create something really powerful.

Writing my experiences down became a positive way to channel all the emotions I was feeling, both over reuniting with Jan and learning to understand my past behaviour in relationship to others. It was incredibly enriching to spend time with Jo and work on a project we were both so passionate about. It was hard work and emotionally draining, but each week I looked forward to our regular Friday sessions, when we spent a few hours together talking and recording our conversations.

As the writing progressed, however, the gap in my story became glaringly obvious. I felt that it would be incomplete if I didn't at least try to fill in some of the empty spaces, even if the search ultimately resulted in a dead end. It was time to front up to Jan and ask for her help. But while she tried to give me the information I was seeking, she struggled to dredge up anything more than what she'd already shared. I showed her the photo I had found of the *Northern Star*. She smiled when she saw it and shared some lovely stories of the fun they'd all had on board, but no matter how hard she tried, she just couldn't remember Bob's surname.

Okay, I thought, was there another way? Jan had said she was sure she had given Bob's full name to the Salvation Army, along with other details relating to him, and she thought a record of this might have been kept. It was worth a try, so I made contact with their Family Tracing Service. The person I spoke to warned me there was a backlog of enquiries, and although they would do their best to find the information, it could be many months before they were able to get back to me.

It actually took almost a year before I got a response, and unfortunately it revealed that many of the records for Redroofs (the facility where I was born) had been destroyed. There was only a one-line entry stating the date my birthmother had entered the home, when she gave birth and when she left.

The Salvation Army suggested that I get back in contact with the Department of Child, Youth and Family Services to see if they had my adoption report on record. By this point I was starting to give up hope, as I presumed the report would state 'Not Recorded' for any details relating to my father, just as it had on my original birth certificate. I applied for it anyway, and when an envelope arrived a short time later, I was surprised to see how thin it was. I had thought there would be a file of some description, so perhaps it was simply a letter telling me there wasn't any further information on record. I didn't feel excited — I just felt quite blank.

Inside was a one-page typed report. There it was in black and white — my father's full name. The next jolt came when I read the description of him, which not only said he was South African (rather than Australian) but that he was 'now married'. Where on earth did that come from? Had Jan known all along that he was married? Surely, she would have mentioned this to me, but how else would it have got in the report unless she had said it? I was in turmoil. Should I call Jan and ask her, or should I just get straight onto the computer and see what I could find out about him? His surname was unusual — I had never heard it before or from where it originated.

While these thoughts were spinning through my head, I realised that I felt quite disassociated from the details in the report. When I had first held my original birth certificate in my hands, I had read Jan's surname and thought, I'm a Harvey, but I didn't have that sort of connection with my birthfather's name. I didn't feel like I had any connection to him at all.

Despite this, I decided to see how far I could go in tracking him down. I started with online directory listings for Australia and South Africa, since these were the only two countries I knew he had a link to. Even though the report had said Bob was South African, I really didn't think Jan would have got that wrong. Perhaps it was an administration error made when the information she gave to the Salvation Army was written up. He had certainly left the boat in Sydney to visit family, according to Jan, so I thought there would be at least some trace of his extended family. Sure enough, there were a dozen listings for Australia that could have been a hit. South Africa only had three listings that matched.

I sat at my desk with the printout of phone numbers in front of me. What should I do? Should I do anything? When searching for Jan, the next step had come and then the next, without much thought about either the process or the consequences. This was different. Even when Andrew got home from work that night, I still hadn't done anything. 'Let's start making phone calls,' he said, but I just couldn't. I wanted to stop and think it through this time. We had been very lucky with Jan, but this man had no idea I existed.

•

For the next week I was pulled in two directions. Part of me kept going back to the few words on the adoption report that had described Bob's personality: kind, thoughtful and considerate. Even though he had let her down badly, Jan had used these words to describe him to the person writing the report. Why would she do that, unless it really was her impression of him? If it were an accurate description, surely he would be open to hearing about me?

Then the other part of me would swing back to the letter he wrote telling Jan he hoped she would 'deal with the problem'. Did I really want to confront someone with the news that the 'problem' hadn't been dealt with in the way he'd thought it had? I had the power to tell him about the existence of his daughter and two granddaughters. Did I have some sort of responsibility to do this? He didn't have any power to find me because Jan had taken that away from him when she had told him she'd had a miscarriage.

In the end, I reverted to my old strategy of believing I was doing this for someone else. I convinced myself that, for now, Bob had no need whatsoever to know anything about me, and I would be doing him a favour by not making contact. My first loyalty was to Jan, and I wanted to be sensitive to her feelings. Despite everything I had learnt about it being okay to have my own needs, I decided it was easier to put them aside. I knew

I was perhaps being a coward, but another part of me decided to be gentle with myself and not push myself to do something I felt so uncomfortable about. The time wasn't right; perhaps it would be at a later stage.

Weeks went by and I felt increasingly awkward about keeping the discovery of Bob hidden from Jan. We had always been honest with each other, so eventually I showed her the report. She was horrified to read the information about Bob being married and was fairly certain she had never said anything along those lines to the authorities. We both speculated that perhaps the adoption officials had found out more about him and the report wasn't solely based on the information she gave them.

I still felt torn. I had found my birthmother and had a wonderful relationship with her, which so many people didn't get to have. She was a fantastic grandparent to my children and adored her son-in-law. I had already found out so much about myself. Wasn't this enough?

But having that little bit of information about my birthfather had reignited a hunger for more that I couldn't shake. There was still someone out there who might look like me. I'm not sure why I was so fixated on this, but I suspected it was part of my deep longing to fit in, and I felt a sense of responsibility to my daughters to access their genetic line. What if one of them came to me one day and said, 'Mum, why didn't you even look for my grandfather and now it's too late?'

I wanted another fairy-tale reunion story — I wanted to phone the first Bob on the list and discover it was the right person, that he was lovely and had all the amazing qualities

Jan first saw when she fell in love with him. I wanted him to embrace me and to answer my questions. I wanted him to have delightful children who looked like me and welcomed me as their sister. That was the fairy tale.

Months went by, and after a particularly intense period of working on the first draft of the book, I suddenly woke up one morning and thought, this is ridiculous, I have to know what happened to him. I hunted out my neglected list of phone numbers and got to work.

The only change from the online search I had run previously was that there was now just one listing with his surname in South Africa, rather than three. Could this be a sign? I was ready to pick up the phone then and there until I realised the time difference meant I would need to wait a little longer. There were also 14 listings with his surname in Australia with either the initial 'B' or 'R' (his full name was Robert), and I felt Australia really was a more likely option given that Bob's family came from there. Even if I couldn't track Bob down, I felt there was a good chance of finding someone related to him.

I hadn't told Andrew what I was planning, but when he came home for lunch that day, I confessed that I wasn't going to let another day go by without trying to make contact with Bob. However, gripping the cold, hard telephone receiver in my hand and preparing to dial was another matter. Nerves and the fear that I would burst into tears at any moment threatened to render me incapable of speaking. Once again, I sweet-talked my lovely husband into taking over, pointing out that he had made such a brilliant job of it last time, he really should be the one to try again.

Despite the success we'd had connecting with Jan at our first attempt, this time my aim was simply to try to track down someone who might know Bob, but unbelievably, the very first call Andrew made to the South African phone number hit the jackpot. The phone was answered by a woman who turned out to be Bob's wife. He was out, but she answered a number of Andrew's questions about Bob's time in South Africa, and his travels during the late 1960s. Andrew told her that he was trying to trace a family member. She suggested he call back in a couple of hours when Bob would be home again.

Andrew and I couldn't believe that it might actually be him. There were so many more variables this time, and the matches to what I had discovered from my adoption report could have simply been coincidences. Andrew offered to call the Australian numbers to see if he could find out more about the family connection there and he dutifully spent the next hour working through the list. Most of the people were very nice and interested in the story, but all leads appeared to be dead ends. Once again, he called the South African number, but the phone connection this time wasn't good and kept cutting out, so he had to ring back several times, which made for a very disjointed conversation.

The cover story Andrew used initially when he spoke to Bob was that he was trying to track down some details for a family tree; however, the nature of his questions quickly raised Bob's suspicions, so eventually Andrew told him the truth — that he was married to someone who thought, based on the evidence we had gathered, that Bob could be my birthfather. Andrew talked about Jan being on the *Northern*

Star when it sailed from Durban to Australia during late 1967. He also told the story of her getting pregnant on the last night of the voyage.

Bob certainly didn't deny it, in fact he told Andrew it was 'quite possible'. Obviously, the whole conversation was a shock to him, but given the circumstances, he was surprisingly forthcoming. He said he had done a lot of travelling during that time, with multiple ship voyages around Australia. He remembered the *Northern Star*, but he also told Andrew that there had been numerous women during that time. Bob also shared that he had gone through a marriage breakup just before leaving South Africa and so had fully enjoyed his newfound freedom. Andrew was surprised at how candid he was, but once he started probing a bit further, Bob admitted that his memory was quite hazy regarding the whole period.

Andrew finally came off the phone and told me he thought we probably had the right person, but there had still been no definite confirmation. Bob couldn't remember, for example, Jan ever writing to him to tell him she was pregnant. Andrew had gained Bob's permission for me to write with more details, so I immediately put together some photos of Jan, myself and the girls, a copy of the adoption report and my birth certificate, plus a long letter explaining my search for Jan and reiterating everything we had discovered about Bob.

I didn't receive a reply from him for a month. His memory, even with the prompting of my photographs, was still sketchy, but he reiterated that his divorce just prior to making the trip home to Australia to see his parents had been difficult, and he'd been in a bit of turmoil at the time around whether to stay in Australia or return to South Africa. He wrote that he still had a menu from the voyage to Australia that included a message signed by 'your Jan'. He admitted that he had felt quite emotional as he read through my letter and realised what he had put Jan through.

He told me a little bit about his life. He had travelled extensively and had met his wife five years after he returned to South Africa. Together they had raised her three children, and in 1978 they had a child together, my half-sister. I was delighted to finally discover that I had a birth sibling, and it was wonderful to discover more about my Australian heritage. Bob described travelling to New Zealand in the mid-eighties and visiting good friends in Wellington and Rotorua. His life seemed busy, very active and happy. I was glad for him — but of course sad for Jan that the brief encounter they had shared, and which had made such a huge impact on her, had barely touched his life.

●

For the next few months, Bob and I exchanged a number of emails. He also told his daughter about me, and she sent several lovely emails telling me all about her life and casting some light on what Bob had been like as a father. Every time a message arrived from either of them, I felt an immense jolt of joy that I finally had this opportunity to connect with another part of my genetic heritage. South Africa was, however, a very long way from New Zealand. Emails were great for fact sharing and getting a feel for them as people through the way they communicated, but I didn't feel comfortable with the idea of picking up the phone to Bob. I was worried that we would find we had little to talk about.

As the months went by the contact became less frequent. I sent a couple of short emails to Bob and received no direct answer, just occasional group emails showing pictures of African animals and funny videos — nothing personal. Is this it? I wondered. The connection was so tentative that I realised it could be broken at any time by a misplaced question or a simple lack of interest. I couldn't see how Bob and I would ever actually meet, as I didn't have any other strong drivers to take me to his part of the world. The travel plans Andrew and I had for when the children were older didn't include South Africa, and as adventurous as Bob had been in his life, with most of his close family in Australia now gone, it seemed unlikely he would make it to New Zealand again. Could we actually have any sort of ongoing relationship without much chance of meeting?

Almost six months after my last message to Bob, an email unexpectedly landed in my inbox. As soon as I saw it my heart leapt, and a huge grin spread across my face. He apologised for the lack of contact and he told me all the things he had been up to in the last few months, including family visits to his stepchildren and travel adventures with friends.

I realised how important that small amount of contact had become to me, and I vowed, just like I had with Jan, not to let it slip away. Perhaps one day we would meet and, if not, I had learnt some things about my birth family that I had never expected to know. My half-sister was ten years younger than me — surely there was a way we could get together at some point. Honesty had always served me well in my relationship with Jan so I felt this was the way forward with Bob. I emailed him back and as well as updating him on everything I had been up to, I asked whether he was interested in hearing details about my daughters — his only genetic grandchildren as far as I knew. It had always surprised me and even hurt a little that he hadn't seemed curious about them in our previous correspondence.

An honest answer came back almost immediately. Bob said he had not consciously avoided asking about them and was interested in everything they were up to, but confessed he found it difficult to relate to them given the circumstances and the distance involved. He offered to make direct contact with them via email to start building a relationship, and he talked about his close ties with his other grandchildren through his stepchildren, particularly two of the girls who were very close in age to my daughters.

Again, a smile spread across my face. He cared! He also reiterated that he would love us to try to visit South Africa one day, and he said he would be delighted to host my family or any friends who happened to be in that part of the world. At that point, Andrew and I made a commitment to somehow find the means to take the girls to meet 'Grandbob' while we still could, given that he was now in his late seventies. Somehow, we would make it happen.

So, after a year of planning and saving, we embarked on a world trip at the end of 2016, with a stop off in Cape Town just before Christmas. For weeks before we left, friends and family kept asking me how I was feeling about meeting my birthfather or telling me I was crazy when they heard that Bob had invited us to stay with him. 'Why not?' I had responded, knowing that if we didn't feel comfortable, we could always move to a hotel. This blasé attitude stayed with me until we were in Johannesburg Airport waiting for our connecting flight to Cape Town. The plane was delayed, and during the wait it finally dawned on me what a completely mad thing I was doing — flying halfway around the world to meet a man who until recently hadn't even known I existed. Someone who had seemingly left my birthmother high and dry when she was pregnant with his child; he could be a monster for all I knew.

As it turned out, Bob and his family could not have been more welcoming. We got to know each other while exploring one of the most beautiful cities I have ever visited, we drank delicious South African wine, shared wonderful meals, went on a luxury safari adventure, and thoroughly enjoyed our introduction to South Africa. Andrew and I particularly connected with my half-sister and her husband, and the girls were embraced as cherished grandchildren.

I can't pretend that parts of the week weren't awkward. On the first night, for example, Bob took me aside and said he had something he felt he needed to tell me. It turned out that I wasn't the only illegitimate daughter in his life. A year after I was born, another child arrived unexpectedly, and although he had supported her financially until she was an adult, at that stage he had never met her, nor had he met her two children. This situation had caused quite a bit of heartache in his family over the years ... but that's not my story to tell.

The week culminated with an incredible evening at my half-sister's house where we celebrated an early Christmas. Loving speeches were given, gifts exchanged, and an emotional Bob gave me the copy of the menu from his last night aboard the *Northern Star*, which had been signed by Jan all those years ago. We flew out of Cape Town believing we might never see Bob again. Amazingly, less than a year later, a great mate of his shouted him a trip to Australia and New Zealand for his eightieth birthday, so we were not only able to welcome the two of them to our home but also hosted a dinner party attended by my cousin — who knew nothing about me until that morning, and who happened to live 20 minutes from us in Hawke's Bay.

Sometimes doing crazy things does pay off. Taking a risk by travelling to South Africa to meet my birthfather in person meant that I opened the door for my children to have an ongoing relationship with their South African family. For me, developing a connection with Bob, no matter how tentative, has certainly added richness to my life. I now know that I have a place in his heart and am wanted by both my birthparents. I also finally found out where my height came from — Bob is well over six feet tall!

Our time in Cape Town and Bob travelling to visit us in New Zealand reinforced to me that having the courage to connect is absolutely worth making yourself vulnerable for. I have of course been extremely lucky with the outcome I've had from reaching out to both my birthparents. I know that this is often not the case.

On a day-to-day basis I still have to juggle the needs of both my birth family and adoptive one, but I am getting better at recognising when I am falling into the trap of being the people- pleaser, rather than figuring out what is right for me. I've got a lot more work to do on myself. I recognise my triggers much more easily now in terms of seeking external validation, falling into habits of perfectionism in order to feel valued, and my desire to control the people and the circumstances around me. Now I need to figure out how to stop these triggers from driving my reactions.

I also recognise that I have a challenge ahead in terms of learning to value myself as a mother and having confidence in my ability to nurture my daughters through their early-adult years. For this reason, at times I have worked with several therapists when the challenges have felt overwhelming. Undertaking personal development to learn to acknowledge and embrace all parts of myself — including the messy bits — is something I have found incredibly useful.

What has been surprisingly validating and empowering for me has been undergoing the process of correcting my name — which, unfortunately, had to be by deed poll. I was told my original birth certificate was illegal. Such is the story of an adopted person: setbacks and feelings of rejection can be lurking, no matter how many years on. However, that initial realisation that my name should be what my birthmother chose to name me has never stopped mattering. Now, I am legally as well as psychologically Brigitta Baker, but you're welcome to still call me Brigs.

In every aspect of my life, slowly I am learning to be kinder to myself. The journey continues.

Above: Me as a baby; at Uncle Ray's wedding, aged ten.
Below: Aged eight, with my younger brother Alex.

PART 2

CHAPTER 6

Are you my mother?

> 'Where is my mother?' he said. He looked for her. He looked up. He did not see her. He looked down. He did not see her. 'I will go and look for her,' he said. So away he went.
>
> — P. D. Eastman, *Are You My Mother?*

My adoption experience appears to be fairly typical of the 1960s in New Zealand. I was adopted by a married couple who were unable to have their own children. While financially they struggled at times, I was raised in a secure, loving and stable family environment.

Mum told me the story that, on the day I was born, she felt unsettled all day. At that stage, she knew nothing about my pending birth, but destiny was about to play a hand in her life.

It was to be a further three weeks before my parents received a call from a social worker telling them that I had been born and was now available for adoption. Mum said she knew in that moment that I was theirs.

Sue, my birthmother, was 17 years old when she discovered she was pregnant. She was dating and in love with my birthfather, Tony, who was 19. I was conceived in late 1958, a time when most unwed mothers were shamed by society and at times disowned by their families, and Sue was sent away to live with strangers, far from the love and support of her family and friends.

Moments after I was born, we were separated. Sue said she knew she had given birth to a girl, but then only had a fleeting glance of me before I was gone. Because I had significant mucous on my lungs, I was transferred from Taihape to a Karitane unit in Whanganui where I spent the first four weeks of my life; neither with Sue nor in the arms of my adoptive parents. When I was healthy, my adoptive parents were informed of my existence, and soon after that call, they arrived to take me to my new home in Piopio, where my father was a Presbyterian minister in a local parish. One other detail about this time was that on the way home that day, we were involved in a car accident that left us all with minor injuries.

•

Dad loved to tell me the story of their first impressions of me. He told me how they arrived at the hospital and were taken by the nurse along a line of babies in the nursery. The nurse pointed to me and said, 'There she is.' Dad said his first thought was, 'Great, we get the ugliest, scrawniest one with a spiky black mop of hair!' Despite my off-putting appearance, they were clearly delighted to take me home, as his words were infused with love and joy. I basked in every re-telling with great delight. Dad used to say that they 'chose' me. This was not technically true; however, it spoke of their desire for me to feel wanted and special. My mother, having been told that she was unable to have children, said they longed for a child and had waited several years for the chance to become adoptive parents. They chose the name Joanne for me because it means 'gracious gift from God' and that's how I felt, cherished and very much wanted.

As a toddler, Mum and Dad said that I was an outgoing, bubbly little girl who was nicknamed 'microgroove' because I seldom stopped babbling away to myself or whomever would give me their attention. I was very proud to tell everyone I was ''dopted', my face beaming as though it were a badge of honour. These stories reinforced a sense of being loved and valued, which led me to feel good about myself and be happy. They were the only stories I recall growing up. There were none about where I came from or why.

Inevitably, when I suffered health issues or needed to have a surgical procedure, my parents struggled with the fact that they had no medical information to offer doctors. I often heard them say, 'We know nothing; Joanne was adopted.' This led to frequent doctors' visits, as they were unsure if the ailment I was complaining about was serious and whether it could be hereditary. Witnessing these conversations felt so uncomfortable. I loathed that being me seemed to make things more difficult or make people feel awkward.

•

Our family moved to Auckland when I was three years old, as Dad had been appointed minister of a larger parish. Soon after this, my parents had to attend a church conference in the South Island and they decided it would be best for me to stay with Nana, Dad's mother, and his brother, whom I had spent little time with prior to this. Mum and Dad were away for the next three weeks. Many years later, as an adult in therapy, a memory of this time with Nana surfaced, accompanied by a flood of feelings that were so intense I felt like my survival was at stake. The therapist explained that these were likely to be the same feelings I experienced as a newborn when separated from my birthmother, then again when in hospital in those first few weeks of life, and now when left at Nana's. In time, I got up the courage to ask Mum if she'd noticed anything when they picked me up after the conference, and after a few minutes reflecting, she acknowledged that I did take some time to warm up to her.

What neither of us understood was that my ability to connect with her in healthy ways had been irreparably damaged by these early experiences. Her acknowledgement gave me permission to blame myself a lot less and to feel the deep sadness and tremendous sense of loss. My heart was heavy about this for some time, and even now traces of these emotions can arise unexpectedly.

Not long after this time spent with Nana, my parents adopted a baby boy. While I have no memories of him coming into our family, I do recall sensing a special bond between him and Mum, which I noticed Mum and I didn't have. Mum and I were quite different people. It was like we had been put together to 'dance' as mother and daughter, yet our rhythms, direction and style were out of step with each other. At times it was simply not pleasant for either of us as we struggled to understand each other's thoughts, feelings, behaviours, and what we needed from the other person. In contrast, I could see that Mum and my brother were quite similar in personality and interests. For example, they enjoyed reading and home-based hobbies whereas I wanted to be out socialising, playing sport and enjoying friends. I recall feeling left out, rejected in favour of my brother and jealous of their closeness, which set in motion a pattern of rejecting Mum by emotionally distancing myself from her and being hard on my brother, belittling him and being verbally cruel. I began spending more time with Dad. I felt loved by and close to him compared to the growing distance between me and my mother.

Starting school began a new chapter. I was out in the world and I vividly remember loving being with other children. I played every sport available, learnt the piano, adored singing in the choir and acting in school performances. Teachers described me as a social, obedient, compliant child during my primary-school years, but one who struggled to concentrate on schoolwork for long periods of time. Mum was a talented dressmaker and sewed beautiful dresses for me to wear to school. Looking back, this was partly due to financial necessity, but also her knowing just how much I loved fashion and looking nice.

It was around this time that I started experiencing stomach problems in the form of pain and vomiting. Frequent visits to the doctor failed to reveal any medical explanation. Enquiry into my medical history again elicited the usual response, that I was adopted. I felt alone with a body that was doing painful things with no explanation or hope of understanding it. A seed of mistrust in myself and my body was sown. This eventually resolved itself but not until I was in my late twenties and embarking upon a personal healing journey.

•

Primary-school years were a major turning point as it was then that I realised being adopted wasn't all about being special and chosen, that it was a different way to enter a family, and one that wasn't anyone's first choice. Nobody else I knew, apart from my brother and me, were adopted. The topic of adoption was rarely talked about outside of my family, so I believed it was some kind of secret life that was not to be discussed. I also became aware that my school friends looked like their parents and siblings. I began to wish for the first time that I, too, looked like someone. My hair was dark like my adoptive parents', but that was where the similarities ended.

My longing to know and to belong somewhere started to increase. I wondered more and more what my birthmother looked like and whether I was anything like her. Was she short or tall, small or large, fair or dark? With no clues as to how I might turn out, I treated my growing body with a sort of curious suspicion — partly wondering and partly worrying what I might end up looking like.

When I was around six years old, my teacher asked us to write a story about ourselves, including where we were born. As I wrote down the name of my birthplace, Taihape, I remember it struck me that I didn't even know where this town was or have any idea how to spell it. Standing up and reading my story to the class, I felt anxious and self-conscious as the words tumbled out of my mouth.

When I finished, I started to sit down but the teacher motioned for me to stay standing, then asked how long I had lived in Taihape. I felt trapped. I hesitated, scanned the faces in the classroom, and felt sick. I had a clear overriding sense that what I was about to say would somehow change the way she and my classmates would see and treat me from then on. I said that I had been adopted, that I'd been born but never lived in Taihape, and that I had spent my first three years in Piopio with my adoptive parents and adopted brother.

This is my earliest memory of feeling shame. Up until then I had been reasonably cocooned from the stigma surrounding adoption at that time, but starting school and being exposed to the world outside of my family brought with it a realisation that there were contrasting stories about adoption. Within my family in those early years, being adopted was special and brought joy, but outside in the world I heard words to describe us that sounded harsh, like 'illegitimate', 'bad blood' and 'bastard', combined with attitudes of secrecy to cover up birthparents' mistakes. It all took its toll on my sense of worth. From then on, I also grappled with the concept that, despite being wanted and loved by one set of parents, I must have been unwanted and therefore unloved by someone else. Feelings of sadness, guilt and rejection surfaced whenever I dwelt on this.

It was a long walk from our house to school. As I trudged along I would often wonder whether something had been wrong with me when I was born, and that this was the real reason I had been given away. I concluded that I must have been a bad baby for my birthmother to come to this decision. Yet I still fantasised about her while walking to school. I would search the faces of women who walked past me and think, 'Are you my mother?' I would imagine her as a beautiful fairy princess, like the ones I read about in stories, which gave me some respite from what I believed to be the hurtful truth.

The questions about who I was and where I came from were never answered during my childhood, when I most needed them to be. I constantly thought about them but rarely asked. It felt clear, for the most part non-verbally, that it was not okay to ask or talk about anything adoption-related.

Around the age of ten, it dawned on me that I must also have a birthfather! I quickly concluded that he mustn't have been a very nice man to leave my mother when she was going to have their baby. I genuinely believed I would never know who he was, so I just shut out any further thoughts of him, and focused my emotional longings and all internal dialogue onto my birthmother. At this stage I still didn't really understand how babies were made, but I knew deep down that somehow the circumstances surrounding my conception and birth were not ideal. As my intellectual capability developed, a new level of understanding about the words 'illegitimate', 'bastard' and 'orphanage' in relation to my own status as an adopted child also developed, but I resigned myself to the fact that nothing I could do or be would ever compensate for my beginnings or my birthparents' misdemeanour.

Prior to going to school, I had been comfortable with people knowing that I was adopted. Now, I felt tarnished by this brush; I wanted to keep it hidden. It was a dark secret and a burden that brought with it intense feelings of aloneness and hopelessness. Much of the time I was able to push these and other related feelings deep down; however, on occasion I simply couldn't contain them, and they would explode out of me. I'd yell 'I hate you!' at my brother and 'You are not my real mother!' at Mum.

Now I can see this behaviour was also fuelled by my jealousy over the emotional connection they had with each other, but at the time it just felt unstoppable. It became a vicious cycle: the outbursts brought relief from my pent-up emotions, but then I would torture myself afterwards with feelings of guilt as I witnessed first-hand the impact my behaviour had on them. Mum would reply mostly with a firm 'I am your mother', then send me to my room as punishment and to calm down. The impact of these outbursts during my adolescent years grew to the point where Mum withdrew her love and attention from me by being silent for days at a time. This rejection was devastating for me on many levels.

The household I grew up in had a strong religious and moral foundation — not surprising given my father's profession as a minister — but the social and cultural context of the time had an equally high moral tone around 'acceptable' behaviour. In our home, the belief that you did not have sex before marriage was certainly reinforced. Every Sunday, while sitting in a church pew, the sense of unworthiness and shame would surface. It made me self-conscious and feel as if the older parishioners were looking at me.

There were also instances when I was told that I should be grateful that I had been 'taken in' by my adoptive family. One such occasion was when my Nana was looking after me and I was misbehaving. She got exasperated and told me that my birthmother had 'come from the gutter', and that I should consider myself a very lucky girl to have been adopted by my parents. She told me that lots of children born out of wedlock ended up in orphanages. Nana would have been devastated if she knew the impact her words had on me. Her comments simply reflected attitudes around adoption in those days, but the pain I felt in that moment reinforced my belief that I was bad, and that other people had a higher status and therefore were more worthy than me. A sense that I needed to do more, give more, be more, in order to compensate for this deficit was born.

I became aware that the feelings and thoughts going on inside me were quite different to what others experienced. As a child, I naturally looked to my parents and other adults for reinforcement about who I was, how I should be, and what was right and wrong. I believed that they knew best. In fact, my father used to play a game where he tickled me relentlessly until I would give in and say, 'Dad, you know best.' But none of these influencers offered anything that would help me make sense of what I was experiencing, so I took on the idea that there was something wrong with me.

The first female figure I trusted and felt at ease around during my childhood was my maternal grandmother. There was a sense of warmth and an earthiness about her, and her hugs and special treats permeated the walls around my heart. When I stayed with these grandparents, each morning after breakfast, Grandma would prepare morning tea for 10 o'clock sharp, as my grandfather expected it. She would toss flour over the kitchen bench, a sign that her delicious scones were in the making. My mouth watered long before they reached the oven. Some days they were cheese, other times sultana or plain. We would watch them rise in the oven, me willing them to hurry up. The wait was worth it. Grandma covered them with lashings of butter and topped them with a great dollop of her homemade raspberry jam. The scones were then washed down with a hot cup of tea laced with a 'sinful' teaspoon of sugar, snuck in by Grandma without my parents' knowledge.

Grandad was a tall man who left his grandchildren dwarfed by his stature, and at times we were fearful of him. My grandparents had 17 grandchildren. Some found him gruff and a bit scary, but I found a soft spot in him and relished this as often as I could. And yet, whenever I got too comfortable with either of them, a thought would pop into my head, like a neon sign, not to get too close, reminding me that as the adopted ones, my brother and I must surely come at the end of the line in terms of our right to their love. My perception of love was that there was a limited amount to go around, and the 15 cousins who shared the same blood as my grandparents were the ones who deserved it, not my brother or me. I was incapable of allowing myself to feel the love that was all around me. I put up walls to protect me from the pain of not belonging, and I didn't question these self-beliefs about not deserving love until much later in life. I clearly did not need anyone else to reject me; I was good at it myself.

●

Just prior to my tenth birthday, my mother had become pregnant after many years of unexplained infertility. I remember her inviting my brother and me to feel her belly as it grew. It was an amazing experience to feel a baby moving in her womb, and I felt close to her even before she was born — but it also made me wonder about being in my birthmother's womb. I was hungry and ached for the closeness and connection I saw developing between my adoptive mother and her unborn child.

When my sister was born, I was thrilled. I loved to watch Mum breastfeed her. I was mesmerised by the connection I saw; it was palpable — their eye contact and the unconditional love flowing between them. This picture filled me with warmth, but also sadness. Something inside me shifted as I recognised the thing I had longed for — the natural nourishing bond between a mother and child — that was missing for me. In a strange way, I felt relieved of a burden. Only much later was I able to comprehend what I was feeling and put words to it, yet I intuitively felt the absence of the close bond between Mum and me, and realised I'd felt responsible for it not being there. Now that I could see she had it with my sister, I no longer had to work hard to receive or to give love.

On the flip side, it was also another nail in the coffin for my self-esteem because it was more evidence that there was something wrong with me. My birthmother had given me up, then my adoptive mother couldn't connect with me, but she could with my brother and sister. I was obviously unlovable and incapable of connecting.

Giving up on a relationship with Mum meant that I stopped wanting and chasing any kind of connection with her, and I think on some level Mum sensed this. My tenth birthday, a few months after my sister was born, was a party I'll never forget. I knew something was different that day as I watched Mum go to a great deal of effort. It was as if she were trying to reassure me or demonstrate that I was still special to her, despite the new baby and their close bond. Perhaps she was trying to compensate for the connection she also felt we didn't share, but I recall a fabulous party: lots of friends, fun games, delicious food, and me proudly wearing a new dress, a present from Nana. I did feel a warmth between us that day; however, this faded when we resumed the normal routine of day-to-day living. I wished we could have talked about how things were, about how hard it had been for us, how we'd tried but couldn't manage to close the gap between us. But how do you talk about something that you can't define, let alone describe?

At intermediate school, teachers began to make more comments about my lack of concentration and wrote in school reports: 'Joanne is easily distracted'. I vividly recall sitting with my chin in my hands, elbows on my desk, gazing out the window across the green fields daydreaming about what my birthmother was like and her wanting to find me. Then feelings of guilt about being ungrateful for the life my adoptive parents had given me would snap me back to reality. I even remember having favourite teachers become fantasy mothers.

The teenage years brought a whole new level of angst as now I struggled to contain or control my emotions, and my family bore the brunt of it: pent-up hurt, dark feelings cascading as verbal abuse at them. I felt powerless to stop, then would be distraught following these outbursts, as I knew any behaviour that diverged from being good and grateful was likely to result in rejection — something I literally perceived to be life threatening in my fragile state. I began to hate myself for this self-sabotaging cycle that I couldn't seem to control.

I went from being a compliant child at primary and intermediate school to a defiant, rebellious adolescent. I began to fall behind in my schoolwork. Teachers kept telling my parents that I could do a lot better, that I didn't work hard enough. From day to day, I still appeared confident and outgoing. I was in leadership roles and excelling at sport, but few would have guessed that on the inside, feelings of isolation, pain and a sense of aloneness were growing, while not knowing anything about my genetic history became even more insistent.

I remember several significant conversations with my grandfather where he commented on my rather long, skinny feet and dark complexion. He used to tease me that I was going to end up being seven feet tall. We would sit together and ponder what sort of blood ran through my veins. Was I part Māori, Italian, or even Indian? I was both intrigued and anxious about these possibilities because it was scary not knowing who or what I would end up looking like. I was grateful to have these discussions, but at the same time, they reminded me that my brother and I were not like others in my family. Genetically we did not belong, and we did not have the same right to know about our origins as they did. And nor did we ever discuss any of it between ourselves.

As I got older, I was rarely able to please my adoptive mother or make her happy and I felt that she didn't get me. She used to say, 'Nobody else thinks that way, Joanne.' I don't remember her cuddling me or telling me that she loved me. I seemed to consistently do and say things that hurt her feelings. When this happened, she would withdraw and sometimes not speak to me for days, leaving me more hurt, confused and feeling worse about myself.

My parents couldn't work out what was going on with me, but in their attempts to manage the situation, they came down harder, with more frequent groundings and being sent to my room. All I needed were answers, some validation of my feelings — even a hug — but sadly, they didn't have any understanding of what I was going through and I felt as if I were coming apart.

I started asking my parents more questions about my adoption — something I hadn't been able to do in the past in case they would think I was being disloyal to them, but my need to know finally overrode these fears. One day I perched on the stainless-steel bench in the kitchen and asked them about my birthmother. To my surprise and relief, my parents responded with understanding and kindness. It was as if they could see how I longed for and needed this information, but because they hadn't been told much at the time I was placed with them, there was little they could disclose. Dad said he wished they'd asked the social workers more questions when they were going through the adoption process. They weren't offered background information and it didn't occur to him then that it would be so important to me in the future.

It must have been hard for my parents to see my angst and not know how to help. Instead, they were forced to fall back on the platitudes that I had heard many times before: how much my birthmother loved me and wanted the best for me to choose to give me to a family to raise.

This wasn't nearly enough to satisfy my needs. In my head I believed them but in my heart it made no sense. If it were for the best, why did it hurt so much and why did I feel so bad? Why was the pain of not knowing so unbearable? I saw my parents' desperation to ease my distress, and at least sharing my longings with them was significant. I felt like we were on the same team and I was less alone.

This search for identity is a common struggle for all adolescents, but for me it was intensified by the lack of knowledge about my origins, making it so much harder to figure out who I was, what I wanted or how to find my place in the world. I have a vivid recollection of sitting in biology class at high school one day, again gazing out the window in my usual distracted way, but this time the fantasies about my birthmother were not light and fleeting but felt gripping and urgent. They needed to be faced.

As I stared into the space between the green field and the blue sky, it became clear just how much this was all affecting me. I saw adoption for the first time from a more adult viewpoint. The seeds of awareness that I was the victim of a deeply flawed system were planted that day, and my determination to seek justice for these wrongs was ignited. Now, I was angry. I felt compelled to advocate for the underdog and support or defend anyone affected by it.

The headmistress at my high school was an older, authoritative woman who had a reputation for being racially prejudiced against the Māori girls. I had witnessed her cruelty, noticing that she seemed to derive a sense of pleasure from publicly humiliating certain students. Following one of these incidents, a group of us decided to protest against her behaviour. As a result, we were suspended from school for a week, but there was also a formal investigation, and six months later, the headmistress was asked to step down from her position and left the school under a cloud of secrecy.

While it was gratifying to channel strong feelings outwardly, being suspended brought with it a stigma and reinforced my 'bad girl' image. However, this experience taught me that if you stand up for what you believe in, justice can prevail. It was so good to express injustice and witness a positive outcome. Several years later, it would be what spurred me on to advocate for change to the closed adoption legislation.

Growing up, and even well into adulthood, my birthday was always the strangest of days. I would not know how I was going to feel. For several days, even a week, leading up to the day, I would feel flat, at a loss and teary, instead of looking forward to it. Part of this stemmed from thinking about my birthmother even more than usual: Was she thinking about me? Did she even remember it was my birthday? Then on the birthday itself, I was buoyed by the celebration and acknowledgments from family and friends. Beneath this, however, I felt sensitive, sad and distant. These feelings were a barrier to being able to feel special, loved or to let in the good. I'm not sure if anyone noticed this, but I certainly was not able to express in words what I was experiencing.

My need to know more about my birthmother just kept growing until it became clear that this was now a desire to find her and understand why she had given me up for adoption. I felt a giant wave of fear about what this might mean — incredible longing colliding with intense anxiety. I convinced myself that I only wanted information, not to actually know her. After all, she had relinquished me and had given up all her rights, but I had a basic human right to know more about myself.

When I was almost 16, I promised myself that I would search for her, but my boyfriend, whom I went on to marry at age 20, convinced me to wait until I was 21. He knew that I was going through turbulent times at home and luckily for me he had the wisdom to see that this was not the right time to add more emotional complexity to my life. Deep down we were also both scared about what we might discover.

The situation at home came to a head not long after this. Throughout my childhood and teenage years, I had longed to own a puppy. I often begged my parents to let me have one but they didn't think I was responsible enough — and their other argument was that we couldn't afford one. I'd collected so many pictures and ornaments of dogs, my bedroom looked like a shrine to them. Looking back, I can see that my obsession with having a dog of my own was about having something safe to love, to connect with, and to love me back unconditionally. I decided to prove to my parents just how responsible I could be and answered a newspaper advertisement to be a dog-sitter for three months while the owners were overseas. I fed and walked it daily, but even at the end of that period, despite me proving that I was responsible and trustworthy, my parents still said no.

On my seventeenth birthday, my close friend, who could see that I simply had to have a dog, bought me a six-week-old red setter puppy. As she had not discussed this with my parents, they were understandably upset and I was firmly told that I couldn't keep it and must give it back to my friend. I was devastated, and something inside me snapped. I was angry and sad. I knew my parents would never get me or understand what I needed.

Several months later, my father and I had an argument that culminated in him telling me that if I didn't like their rules, I could leave. His comment was half-hearted, but I did. My parents thought that I would come home when I had calmed down. As I walked out that day, I wasn't to know that I would never choose to live at home again.

The pain of what I perceived as rejection hurt me so deeply that I wanted to cut the cord with them. I moved in with a friend's family, who were very supportive and understanding, but I was also in complete emotional turmoil and I could see that something significant had changed. My internal sanctuary of playing out fantasies about my birthmother continued to the point where I truly believed the only thing that could fix me now was to find out more about her.

I couldn't wait to start searching.

CHAPTER 7

The search for self

> Searching is a critical means by which to heal the primal wound and calm the anxiety which manifests itself in a variety of self-limiting or self-destructive behaviours.
>
> — Nancy Newton Verrier, *The Primal Wound*

I'm not sure why 21 was significant, but I had made the commitment to my now husband, Lawrie, that I would wait until then to begin the search. Perhaps we felt I would be mature enough to deal with whatever the outcome of my search might be. Lawrie had promised to help and support me, and I knew he was right to want to wait until I had the resilience to cope with what we might discover.

In the meantime, I began to campaign for change to the closed adoption law. The Adoption Act had governed adoption practice in New Zealand since 1955. This legislation sanctioned the social and cultural attitudes of the time: the belief that a complete separation between birthparents and their adopted child was best for all parties concerned. As a result, all adoption records were sealed. However, groups such as Jigsaw Inc. were starting to lobby for an amendment to the Act. This voluntary organisation held a register with names of adopted people and birthparents who were interested in information about it or wanted to contact each other. The register was based on the birth date of the adopted person. In 1977, Jigsaw petitioned Parliament for a law change, but it would take another eight years for this change to occur.

Growing up in a home and church environment where conversations about issues of social injustice were commonplace meant I could clearly see the injustice of not being afforded the same respect and rights as my non-adopted peers, to not know my history, my stories, to not have the same information that would give me a sense of wholeness, value and worth. While my anger grew, campaigning for change became a positive vehicle for channelling these emotions.

•

When I was 19, I moved to Wellington to be with Lawrie, who was studying at university. I worked as a personnel clerk in the Manners Street Post Office alongside training to be a volunteer social worker. I found out about an adoption support group and started attending the meetings. It was here that I first heard birthmothers sharing their experiences, and showing their pain and fears about the possibility of being rejected by their children. This was something I hadn't even contemplated before, as so far it had been all about me, my pain and my fears. I also heard someone refer to Jigsaw. Up until then I had believed there was no way of searching for information about my adoption. It was a long shot but at least I now had hope and a place to start. Would my birthmother be looking for me?

It seemed like everything was gearing me towards doing something about it. I remember at one point, a number of people, including work colleagues, told me they had seen a woman who looked just like me at various locations around Wellington, including several reports of her catching a bus near my work. I was intrigued and wanted to find this mysterious woman. Could she be related to me?

As my birthday approached, and the commitment to search became real, I began to get very anxious. I had waited so many years to take this step, but now that I was on the precipice of doing so, I was petrified about what I might find or that I would be rejected again. Despite these feelings I wrote a letter to Jigsaw expressing my interest in going on their register. I remember walking to a local post box to send it; as the letter slipped through the slot I was overwhelmed with panic and desperately wanted to retrieve it. I felt sick; I had started something I might not be able to control. What if my birthmother didn't want me? What if the information showed I had been born because of rape or something similar?

It was too late to change my mind. The letter had gone. The next day, on my birthday, a friend called and said, 'Jo, have you seen the *Dominion Post* this morning?' When I told him

I hadn't, he excitedly explained that he had been reading the newspaper on the train into Wellington and had seen an advertisement in the notices section with my birth details. The notice read:

> Born Taihape 15/9/1959
> Happy 21st birthday to you from your birth family.

I couldn't breathe. I heard myself say, 'This can't be true', then fear slowly subsided as I managed to think straight. I saw that in offering me birthday wishes in the newspaper, my birth family were not about to reject me. I never in my wildest dreams imagined this scenario. Oh my goodness, they wanted me! They were looking for me! The notice contained contact details for Jigsaw and invited me to write to them through the agency. Since I had just posted my letter the day before to the exact same address, there was nothing else to do. I just had to wait.

Within a week a letter arrived to say there was a match. What I didn't know at the time was that the person who had received my letter at Jigsaw was actually my paternal grandmother. Incredibly, she was the one who then wrote back to me, and followed up with a phone call to make arrangements for a meeting. At this stage she didn't give away who she really was. I simply presumed she was a representative from Jigsaw, but little did I know after I put down the phone that I had just spoken to my first blood relative.

On the day that we were due to get together, I decided I would meet her on my own, but the phone rang and a new person told me that she was a representative from Barnardos, a social services agency, and that she was going to come and see me instead of the person I had spoken to from Jigsaw. This change of plans sent my anxiety through the roof and I reached for a cigarette. Thoughts whirled around my mind: Why was Barnardos getting involved? What might have gone wrong? Didn't they want to meet me now? When the social worker arrived at my house, I made her a cup of tea and we sat down and this was when she told me the truth — that in fact it was my birth grandmother whom I had spoken to at Jigsaw.

I felt like I was going to faint. I couldn't take it all in. My grandmother was looking for me. Not my birthmother? According to the social worker, she had joined Jigsaw many years earlier in the hope of one day finding me. I recalled a vague memory — at the time my parents had adopted me, they had been told that the paternal grandmother had not been happy about the adoption, and that they needed to 'cover their tracks'. Had she been looking for me ever since? The social worker explained that my grandmother decided at the last minute it would be unfair to turn up to the meeting without my knowing who she really was. As I tried to process everything, she then said that my grandmother was waiting in a local motel, hoping I would still want to meet with her. What could I say? I felt pressured but, as she had driven all the way from Auckland to Wellington to meet me, I didn't feel I could say no.

I agreed for my grandmother to come to our home the next day. I endured another anxious night of waiting. Emotionally it felt like I had entered a kind of vortex; my familiar world was receding, and a new landscape was emerging that I had little choice in or control over. This left me feeling extremely vulnerable. Why was my grandmother the one who was searching? What had happened to my birthparents? Was there something terrible she needed to tell me about them?

The following evening my grandmother Peggy knocked on the door. As I opened it, I remember searching her face for a resemblance. I didn't find it. What I saw was an attractive older woman, stylishly dressed and beautifully spoken. I suddenly felt awkward and didn't know what to do. I had written to Jigsaw hoping to find my birthparents; instead my grandmother was standing in front of me. We went into the lounge and she began to tell me the story of my birthparents. She said they had met at a dance in Wellington and fallen in love. She handed me photos of each of them and I could see a likeness, then she showed me a photo of them dancing in each other's arms at a ball together.

A complex mix of emotions washed over me — relief that the search was over, elation at the image of them looking so happy together, but also sadness at the thought of what must have followed this happy scene. These people were my birthparents!

My grandmother said that her son knew she was meeting with me, but my birthmother had not yet been contacted. She thought she was living in Australia but she wasn't sure how my birthmother would feel about the news that I had been found.

Disappointment hit me. My birthmother hadn't been searching for me at all. Rejection crept in. For all those years my dream had been that *she* was the one looking for me. That my grandmother had been searching did feel like a compliment, but it did not compensate for the fact that my birthmother had not been. My longings had all been focused on her. She was the one I'd fantasised about, the one I had dreamed of being reunited with.

As a child I had formed a belief based on the social norms of the era that my birthfather was a bad man who had abandoned my birthmother when he found out she was pregnant. I never imagined for one minute that I would first know who he was, let alone meet him or members of his family.

I tried to swallow my disappointment. Here was my grandmother, wanting to know all about me and sharing information about my birth family. I remember looking at her, noticing her movements, every nuance in her voice, clinging to these stories about my entrance into the world. I savoured every word. They resonated like a beautiful song touching my heart. Thoughts of my birthmother and fears as to why she might be missing from this picture could wait.

CHAPTER 8

Reunion reality bites

> The experiences of those who have had reunions make one thing clear. No one experiences the reunion that they fantasised about.
>
> — Julie Jarrell Bailey, *The Adoption Reunion Survival Guide*

Following our first meeting, Peggy and I exchanged letters — two strangers getting to know each other and the lives we each led. I found my grandmother to be a very open-minded person with a calm, confident presence about her. She was kind, yet held strong opinions. I looked forward to opening the letterbox and seeing a crisp white envelope with her distinctive elegant writing on it, and I'd read them over and over, searching for any information I may have overlooked. I've kept every one of her letters.

Peggy arranged for me to come to Auckland to meet Tony, my birthfather, and to stay at her house for the weekend. Lawrie and I drove from Wellington. As I entered her home, I soaked up everything I could from the surroundings: the art, the pottery, the books, the photos, the antique furniture. And last but not least, her dachshund, Pansy. Everywhere I looked left me with a sense of connection — much of it was of similar taste to mine, and I hadn't had that experience before.

Arrangements had been made for Tony's sister to pick us up and drive us to his house close by. I was so nervous about meeting these birth relatives after 21 years of not knowing anything about them and overwhelmed at having little time to process any of it. I wished that I knew another adopted person who was going through what I was. Lawrie was a rock throughout this time; however, what I really needed wasn't available. No books or roadmaps for this terrain. Nothing to guide or to reassure me that I would come out the other side of this intact or without sabotaging it in some way.

As we drove up Tony's long gravel driveway, the sun was beginning to set. Looking up at the house, it felt like time was standing still. There was also an element of subterfuge to the whole situation; I had fleeting thoughts that none of my adopted family knew what I was doing. Very few of my friends were aware either.

Tony was standing alone on the veranda and I can remember thinking, 'Thank goodness Lawrie is with me.' My first impression was that he was tall and dark — like the prince in a fairy tale. Tony reached out his arms to embrace me but my body tensed up and I felt very uncomfortable, not knowing how to respond. I remember then sitting on the couch between him and Lawrie and he'd often touch my hand and hold it at times during the evening and I just didn't know how to deal with it. Part of me thought, 'This is my father and it feels wonderful to have him close,' but another part of me thought, 'He's a stranger and I don't know or trust him.'

Tony said that his wife and children were out of town. I was relieved that I didn't have to meet them at the same time; our attention could just focus on each other. Lawrie kept the conversation going and I was grateful for that because it helped keep things light and almost superficial, which was exactly what I needed. I have few other memories of that night, except when Tony dropped a bombshell, just before we left — my birthmother had been contacted and was flying into Auckland from Sydney the next day to meet me. My heart began to race. I tried not to panic, but the feeling of being even more out of control enveloped me. I could hardly breathe.

I had longed to meet my birthmother for as far back as I could remember and now here was my chance, but this scenario left me feeling like I didn't have a choice because she was coming all this way. I couldn't back out now. That panicked feeling of wanting to retrieve the letter I'd sent to Jigsaw now seemed like a premonition. My deepest fear, that sending it would result in me being engulfed by something I couldn't control, was exactly what was unfolding.

Tony was talking about the plans he had made for the next day. He would pick Sue up from the airport around midday and then take her to a motel. Lawrie was given the address and we were to meet them there. My head was spinning. I wanted to throw up. It seemed too unbelievable to be true. But in those days, someone making the effort to fly in from

Australia at short notice was huge — there was no way I could say no.

I don't think I slept a wink that night. Despite wanting this reunion for so long, I honestly felt I wasn't ready to meet my birthmother. My predominant thought was, 'How on earth am I going to get through this?' My only coping mechanism, the one I had used since I was a child, was to suppress my real feelings in the hope that they would diminish or go away.

•

The next morning, Peggy and I spent time going through family photos, and she used them to 'introduce' me to the extended family members. She said that it had come as a huge shock to Sue when Peggy had telephoned her with the news that she had found me. Peggy intimated that she wasn't sure Sue would actually come. All of this just added to my anxiety. Then it was time for Lawrie and me to drive to the motel. We arrived a few minutes before they did and wandered aimlessly around the room. Then they were there, and as Tony and Sue stood in the doorway, the first thing that struck me was how petite, youthful and attractive my birthmother was. I remember walking towards the two of them thinking, 'These are my parents.' It was surreal.

I hugged Sue, but I don't remember how it felt because I wasn't in my body as such. I recall feeling numb, and I can't remember what it felt like to be held by her. Tony put his arms around both of us and said something like, 'This is the family that might have been.' His words sent a shudder down my spine. A poignant reflection of what had *not* happened, followed by a sense of loss.

On the surface, it appeared that Sue was coping okay. We chatted together about how alike we were — seeing similar mannerisms and likenesses was delicious, and a part of me revelled in putting together some of the missing pieces. We spent a few hours with each other, but at the end of that time, we were all emotionally drained. We agreed that I would go back to my grandmother's to have a rest, freshen up, and meet them both for dinner. Tony would stay with Sue. I didn't want to leave. It felt as if I was going to miss out and, in a small way, I felt a bit excluded. Perhaps if I had met Sue on my own, I wouldn't have felt that way. I so wanted time with her on my own, and I was conscious that every minute was precious as she was only here for the weekend; I might not get this opportunity again.

But we agreed, and Lawrie and I drove back to Peggy's house and waited for the telephone call to confirm that Sue and Tony were ready to go out to dinner. I just couldn't wait to get back to them. But when the call came, it was to say that there would be no dinner together that evening. Tony explained that Sue wasn't in a good emotional state and simply wasn't up to seeing me again.

I was truly devastated, but tried not to sound it over the telephone. It was clear that meeting me had brought up a tsunami of historic and buried emotions, and that it was too much for her to process. The wounded side of me interpreted this as rejection and my mind raced with familiar thoughts: 'I'm not good enough. I'm not enough for her to want to see me again.' I tried to rationalise it, but tears fell. Peggy was so supportive and kind. She held me in a warm embrace while I sobbed as if my heart were about to break. The pain was so intense. After some time, I was able to soothe myself with the belief that I would see Sue in the morning.

But that was not to be, either. Sue felt she couldn't cope with it all, and she flew back to Australia that day without seeing me again. This tiny, fleeting window of opportunity with Sue wasn't nearly enough to quell all my years of hunger for her. She had left a card, a beautiful gold chain with a delicate key set with a diamond for my twenty-first birthday, and a framed photograph of herself, which she gave to Tony to give me. Receiving these gifts, which she had obviously taken great care to choose, was special, but it didn't make up for how devastated and hurt I was that she had left without even saying goodbye.

Lawrie and I drove out of Auckland that afternoon. I cried most of the drive back to Wellington. I felt rejected, vulnerable and heartbroken. These feelings were to play out in the relationship I had with Sue for the next 16 years. This was not how I dreamt it would be. I wanted to be close to her, but it was painful and risky.

I had been hurt when she gave me up, and I had been hurt again upon reunion.

CHAPTER 9

The after-effects

> The primal wound, a wound which is physical, emotional, psychological, and spiritual. The ultimate loss and rejection, and an experience which has life-long consequences.
>
> — Nancy Newton Verrier, *The Primal Wound*

For the first three or four months, I tried to integrate the reunion experience and absorb this long-awaited knowledge I had received. I was also tentatively navigating new birth-family relationships and wishing I had someone to talk to who had been through a reunion of this kind.

It was an emotionally exhausting time and continued to be for the next couple of years. There were such highs when letters arrived from members of my birth family — what I now know as the 'honeymoon period' with each of my birthparents, when I felt drawn to be with them all the time. It came from such a deep longing to catch up on the years I had been without them.

I couldn't get enough of these people who were a lot like me, and their familiar mannerisms and ways of thinking. For most of my childhood I had felt like a square peg in a round hole; now I'd found a place where I finally belonged. I relished it and began to find myself through these new relationships. At the same time, I was also grappling with the impact of Sue not coping after our first meeting. The experience of her leaving abruptly without seeing me again and with no explanation left me to misinterpret her reaction. This created significant pain. I knew I had to work through it in order to heal and have her in my life, but it was not going to be easy.

Neither of us had been prepared for reunion. Sue had felt bullied into meeting me by Peggy and Tony. She later said she had closed the door and shut away that part of her life, with no intention of opening it again. For me, I'd had no contact with her, had never even spoken to her before we met, and there was simply no way I could prepare myself for it. I've often wondered whether we might have been able to handle the reunion better if we'd first had time to get to know each other through letters and phone calls. Instead, the intensity of the experience overwhelmed us both. Sue reacted by leaving, and, at only 21, I didn't have the maturity or ability to rise above my pain to see any of it from her perspective. I couldn't understand that her reaction was to do with her own repressed grief and loss rather than it being about me. All I felt was rejection.

I was caught between yearning for a connection with Sue while fearing how vulnerable to rejection this left me. The opportunity to develop our relationship after she went back to Sydney was also complicated by the physical distance. For many years, we only saw each other once or twice a year. Sue's mother, Shirley, lived in New Zealand, and she would come over from Australia regularly to visit her. She would usually let me know when she was coming and intimated that it might be possible for us to meet. I recall the anticipation and excitement I would feel waking up on the day I knew she was arriving into the country. Then, nothing. The days would drag by as I waited to hear from her. I would have done whatever it took to see her, even just for an hour. Often, I received a telephone call from the airport as she was leaving to say she was sorry not to have had time to catch up with me.

Each time I put the telephone down after these conversations, part of me lost hope — hope that I would ever feel whole; hope that I would ever feel the connection and belonging I craved. Then I would battle feelings of rejection and unworthiness until I reached a place of resignation: I was not important or of value to her or to my adoptive mother. I was of not much worth at all. I was reminded of a Buddhist saying: A person's effort reflects their interest in you. What efforts were being shown by them?

○

I visited Sue in Sydney from time to time in the early years of our relationship. I would take someone with me because I didn't feel emotionally strong enough to be with Sue on my own. I would either ask Lawrie or my closest friend, Debbie, to come with me; both had been my security blankets throughout this tumultuous journey.

What I didn't realise at the time were the unconscious processes at play: mine was an innate longing for the mother–

child connection that had been lost at birth; Sue's was the pain that she'd buried long ago, brought again to the surface when she was with me. I found that when we were together, she was nice to me but she kept me at a distance. Often when I would feel that we were getting closer, she would pull away. For some time, the child in me would believe this pulling away was my fault, and it triggered old insecurities. It was many years before I understood that she needed to — not intentionally — shut me out because that's what she'd done in order to survive after she relinquished me for adoption.

For the first 16 years of our relationship, it was me who put in most of the energy and maintained contact, but then perhaps I was the one needy for connection. Debbie believed that my relationship with Sue had always been on Sue's terms, and while it was a shock to hear this, I knew it was true. I was grateful that Sue was willing to be in my life, and I accepted whatever terms suited her. I couldn't bear to lose her again. Debbie once wrote about this post-reunion period, 'Being adopted was what made Jo who she was. Every conversation, every hurt, every longing was about this aspect of her. I remember every birthday, every Mother's Day, there would be this big build-up for her, and she would set herself up for a fall. She was just wanting contact with Sue.'

●

More recently, Sue moved back to New Zealand to look after her mother, whose health was failing. Family get-togethers would be held, and Sue might mention them afterwards.

I recall Sue going to stay with her brother once for a family gathering and her saying, later, 'Oh, I could have taken you, Jo.' I was hurt and perplexed that she still didn't view me as part of the family or wasn't willing to let them meet me. I would have loved to have met my aunts, uncles, cousins. Then I'd push those feelings aside, telling myself that I didn't have the right to expect to be included. There are no maps or guidelines for what to expect in birth-family relationships.

Many times over these years I came close to letting go of our relationship. My hopes would be raised and I'd think, yes, we could have a close relationship, then they'd be dashed in a heartbeat when it didn't happen. These highs and lows impacted heavily on my wellbeing and my family. It seemed that my only option was to give up and no longer pursue it. It was no longer simply the pain of having been separated from Sue at birth, now it was the pain of being separated from her when we were in the same room.

As a therapeutic exercise for myself, I sat down and wrote Sue a lengthy letter expressing how I felt. I poured the pain and anger onto the pages, knowing I had no intention of sending it. A therapist had suggested this to me as a way to process the pain, express unsaid feelings and integrate the experience so that I could let it go and move forward. As I wrote, tears flowed. I grieved the loss of the dream I'd held for most of my life of being close to my mother. I accepted this wasn't to be.

Finally, I could let go and move forward.

For the next two years, which was during Sue's marriage breakup, we didn't have a great deal of contact. I stopped initiating it. Then the balance seemed to change. Sue came out the other side of this period more emotionally available to me than she had been. But in the 37 years since our reunion, I have never truly confided in Sue about my feelings. The relationship always felt too fragile, and I was not prepared to take the risk of damaging what we did have, or worse, losing her. I didn't feel I had the right to ask anything of her. My fear was that she could disappear out of my life again the way she did after that first meeting. These fears subsided over time as Sue became more open and even started to feel and behave like a mother figure to me.

Now we are in an authentic, healthy relationship that is good for both of us, without the patterns of the past undermining it.

Through counselling, I have reached a much greater understanding of why Sue responded to me the way she did in the early years of our relationship. I no longer go down the well-worn path of rejection. I am able to say to myself, 'It's not about me.' Sue has given me lots of messages in recent years about how much she loves me, so I now choose to reflect on the good aspects of our relationship.

●

During those difficult years with Sue, my birthfather was a strong support. I'm not sure Sue and I would have the relationship we do today without Tony helping me to understand how her experience of giving me up shaped how she was with me. I always looked forward to spending time with Tony. I think part of the reason was that I had no expectations of him. Because I never thought for a minute that I would meet my birthfather, everything I received from him and from my grandmother was a bonus, whereas I had fantasised for as long as I could remember about meeting my birthmother. I took those longings, expectations and unmet needs into the relationship with Sue and it nearly cost us what we have today.

There were still times, however, when I would be at a family gathering with Tony, and while enjoying being part of it, I was conscious that I didn't have an automatic right to be there. From time to time I would hear about other family events that I hadn't been invited to and I would feel a little hurt, but the ability to rationalise this was easier than when it happened with Sue. It didn't happen often; most of the time I was included, and I felt lucky to feel so welcome.

Through the early phase of reunion with Tony, I noticed a kind of physical attraction towards him. This phenomenon, which sometimes occurs between adopted people and their birthparents, is known as 'genetic sexual attraction' and usually happens between close relatives who first meet as adults. Nothing had been written about it at the time I met Tony, but it has now been acknowledged as quite a common experience. Adopted people and their parents can experience feelings of attraction when they reconnect as adults that are so strong and intense, they can be interpreted as sexual desire. I talked to Tony about it years later and he said that he didn't reciprocate what I had felt.

It was easy to see Tony as a friend during these early years, and we had fun and bonded through the shared experiences. Over time I came to see him as more of a father figure, although I never had any expectations of him being one. But

I feel blessed to have two amazing and loving fathers in my life, and different, unique relationships with each of them. Tony didn't try to parent me; he just gave his opinion, while my adoptive father continued in the parenting role. Also, Tony treated me similarly to his other three children, which I appreciated. They were quite young when I first came into their lives, so they grew up knowing me as part of their family. I felt accepted and, although we are different people, I have forged a good relationship with each of them and settled into a fairly normal way of being a family.

CHAPTER 10

Waking up

> Owning our story can be hard, but not nearly as difficult as spending our lives running from it. Embracing our vulnerabilities is risky, but not nearly as dangerous as giving up on love and belonging and joy — the experiences that make us most vulnerable. Only when we are brave enough to explore the darkness will we discover the infinite power of our light.
>
> — Brené Brown, *The Gifts of Imperfection*

Here I was, at 27 years old, looking out over the landscape of my life. On the surface it appeared as though I were living my dreams. I was married to my high-school sweetheart and had two beautiful, healthy children, we had purchased our first home and I was beginning a new career in social work. My relationship with my adoptive parents was good, and I had been reunited with my birthparents.

So, why was I such an emotional and psychological wreck? Intermittent bouts of mild anxiety and bone-deep sadness had now magnified into panic attacks that were terrifying, overwhelming and paralysing. My doctor diagnosed them as post-natal depression, triggered by the birth of our daughter. I began to make excuses to avoid leaving the house because when I did, I was filled with fear that I would have another attack and not be able to care for my children.

I accepted this diagnosis at the time, in the absence of any other explanation. However, whether it was or it wasn't, upon reflection I came to understand it as my inner authentic self or soul endeavouring to wake me up to the reality that I was not living a life true to myself — I had never been in a loving, trusting relationship with myself. I had not listened to my heart, my longings or my intuition. I rarely expressed my feelings in life-affirming ways or valued my own needs to meet them. I had long-abandoned myself, and this needed to change. All that I'd buried and the early trauma I'd repressed for years came to a head. My self-protective mechanisms could not hold back the tidal wave of emotions any longer.

I was now driven by a need to understand what I was experiencing, to find answers to ease the intense pain and vulnerability I felt, and to discover how to change it. I started reading writers and theorists in the fields of philosophy, science, psychology, and Eastern and Western spiritual traditions. They became a reassuring light accompanying me through a long dark tunnel, and they gave me the courage to turn towards myself, instead of away.

I had written a journal since the loss of my adoptive grandmother when I was 16, but now I began writing in earnest. I became curious about the rationality of my thinking and the stories I told myself, and the pages revealed an accumulation of irrational, inaccurate and negative beliefs rather than empowering truths. But I also learnt that I had an inner strength to cope with whatever I would discover or emotionally trigger. I knew I had just scratched the surface and was ready to accept I was someone who, despite having been lucky, had issues and challenges.

I attended a personal-development workshop called Finding Oneself. Despite every cell in my body screaming *don't go*, something kept moving me towards what I hoped would lead me out of the fog. As I listened to other people's stories, I felt relieved and comforted to discover I wasn't the only one out there struggling. I shared with the group how I had experienced a 'good' adoption and was fortunate to have been reunited with my birth family, but I was experiencing anxiety. By the end of the workshop, it was clear that for my healing, I needed to take responsibility for my life, and stop blaming myself and others — a habit that always left me with a sense of hopelessness and as if I were a victim.

Despite continuing with self-help and reading books and writing on personal development, I found little written on the experience and impact of being adopted. The writings of Carl Jung, the Swiss psychiatrist and psychoanalyst, affirmed that the answers we are seeking are within us, although his theory was not the quick fix I would have liked. It turned out I'd embarked upon a journey similar to that outlined in *The Hero's Journey*, a term coined by academic and mythologist Joseph Campbell, where the ordinary person goes on a personal quest, overcoming fears, facing challenges and being tested. They are usually rewarded in the form of knowledge, insight, realising their potential, living an authentic, fulfilling life and sharing their wisdom with others.

One of my early insights was that I was seeking love, connection, validation, acceptance and belonging, but always through other people and external events. Regardless of why I may not have received these, I would conclude it was because I was not worthy, not deserving, and I'd feel abandoned. This triggered a negative internal dialogue, thoughts of self-rejection and loathing that could play for days, even weeks, at significant cost to my self-esteem and wellbeing. So, I placed my entire worth and right to exist or be happy in the hands of others, and I was responsible for the self-sabotaging patterns that kept me from what I desperately longed for and needed in order to be psychologically healthy.

It was years later that I made the connection that this pattern originated from the primal wound at the time of separation from my birthmother, and that this was nature's mechanism to protect a dependent, vulnerable infant in this situation. While I felt my first flickers of possibility, hope and motivation, I had no idea how to go about changing things. Again I felt overwhelmed. This pattern was all I had known. Who was I or who would I be without it?

Around this time, I attended a workshop on diary journalling, based on the book *The New Diary* by Tristine Rainier. Journal writing had already provided me with a safe place to allow emotions to surface and helped process raw, unedited feelings such as rage and hopelessness before they spilt out on those closest to me. Could it offer more? During the workshop,

I learnt not to judge my thoughts or feelings but to be curious and kind towards them, to use the journal to capture and record dreams and longings and to set goals and record passages that spoke to me from books I was reading. We were encouraged to creatively express whatever came to the surface, then to close our journals and to return to it another time, in order to read the contents from an objective and reflective stance.

Beginning to see the writing as a 'trusted, kind and wise companion' empowered me to respect the words on the page. At times they woke me up to deep truths — that there was a clear connection between my adoptive experience, the way I felt inside, my lack of self-love, low self-worth and the limiting beliefs and patterns blocking me from being my real self and from living my own life. Waking up to these unconscious patterns and self-protective mechanisms was transformational and life changing, while the awareness and a growing sense of trust guided me towards a more respectful and kinder relationship with myself.

●

Meanwhile, after years of lobbying for the adoption records to be opened, it finally came to fruition. In New Zealand, in 1985, the Adult Adoption Information Act became law, and adopted people and birthparents had access to information and a process through which to contact one another. I was grateful that society was finally acknowledging the injustice of the closed adoption system. The new amendment meant that adopted people were entitled to the same human rights as those who were not adopted, and birthparents were entitled to know what happened to the children they relinquished. Shame would no longer be the driver of secrecy.

I wanted to be part of this new landscape. I applied for and was appointed as an adult adoption social worker with the Department of Social Welfare. My role in those early days was to counsel adopted people who had applied for their original birth certificates and birthparents who wanted to be reunited with their children. The counselling allowed them to ask questions and receive advice regarding searching and making contact. While it did offer some support, in hindsight, it was a naive and superficial offering as it addressed only the tip of the iceberg in terms of deeper trauma.

Over the next 24 years, I worked in various roles within national and international adoption services. I look back on my work as being an immense privilege, although there were times when the emotional nature of the work combined with my own development and reunion process was psychologically taxing and a significant stretch. While I was feeling stronger at this point, I still wanted to learn more so that I could help myself and my clients to change entrenched patterns and behaviours. Awareness alone isn't enough. The motivation to continue working towards becoming a whole person, a better parent, partner and professional, outweighed any resistance to counselling.

In June 1996, I noted in my journal: 'My therapist provided a safe environment and a gentle guiding hand to face and work through blocks and challenges, edging me towards more self-awareness, as I connected with, expressed, and integrated the deeply buried emotions of abandonment, rejection and grief.'

Then I read the work of Nancy Verrier, an American clinician and adoptive mother. In *The Primal Wound: Understanding the Adopted Child*, she explains that her research revealed a wounding takes place in an infant's psyche as a result of being separated from the birthmother. I also came across the writings of John Bowlby, a pioneer in the field of attachment theory. Bowlby defines attachment as a 'lasting psychological connectedness between human beings'. He suggests that for a child, abandonment is experienced as a kind of death, not only from the loss of the mother but also of the 'child-self', the core of our being, the part that allows a person to feel whole. He surmises that this leaves a lifelong legacy that plays out in recognisable patterns, something Verrier identifies as seven core issues: abandonment/rejection, loss, grief, shame/guilt, identity, intimacy and control.

Verrier and Bowlby's rigorous and evidenced-based studies acknowledge what society perhaps has not: that there is a life-altering and potentially life-limiting impact from separating a mother and her child.

The clarity and accuracy of their findings cracked open what was left of my own shell of denial. I felt a palpable sense of liberation; it wove its way through the nakedness and vulnerability I was feeling. In that moment, I was wide awake to seeing how my self-worth, self-image and life choices had been based on a core belief that I was bad, and that that was the reason for my birthmother's decision to give me away and why I did not connect or feel close to my adoptive mother. Up until then I had thought, something is wrong with me; it is all my fault.

These theories revealed that I was responding in predictable ways. In relationships, I was caught up in limiting patterns of behaviour, designed to protect me from being rejected or abandoned again. But the emotional residue of feeling bad culminated in further patterns of behaviour: striving to be perfect, to people-please, to be, do and give more than others were expected to, in order to compensate for my deficit. The acknowledgement of a primal wound and its legacy began to loosen my grip on this belief system. I caught a glimpse of an answer to a question I often asked myself: Why can't I be happy like my husband and non-adopted friends?

I contacted a therapist and booked a session to process this knowledge and its psychological impact more fully. I remember, at one unintentional moment, I felt I was going to die; everything went pitch black. I couldn't see, couldn't breathe, couldn't speak, I literally couldn't move. The therapist kept talking calmly, gently guiding me until I regained some semblance of equilibrium, but the somatic traces of this experience left me in a dissociated fog for several days. I had triggered my original wound of separation that had been locked in the unconscious part of my psyche.

As I delved further into the findings of Verrier and other clinicians, I began to see that the feelings from the primal wound trauma had been showing up in daily life as anxiety, anger, hyper-vigilance, and a fear of rejection and loss. Verrier suggests that during childhood, the trauma is often unconsciously projected onto the mother figure raising us, in the form of verbally abusive behaviour towards her. My adoptive mother had unwittingly brought on and experienced a great deal of this during my adolescence. Sadly, neither of us understood why at the time, leaving us at a loss as to what was happening or how to change it.

●

My time spent in therapy was invaluable. Telling my story to someone trustworthy, who gave me acknowledgement and objective feedback, brought with it a whole new level of awareness and clarity that I did not experience from solely writing in my journal. Despite the work and the pain, the presence, deep listening, empathy and compassion I received from the therapist was like the afterglow from stepping out of a deliciously warm bath, where all the tension has melted away. Parts of me, long buried, began to surface as the walls around my heart softened. The unconditional, empathic relationship my therapist offered became the rich soil for growing trust in myself and others. I learnt how to turn towards and relate to myself in this same way, instead of turning away, full of self-criticism, judgement and rejection. I was able to slowly let in some of the warmth that had always been there waiting.

Doing the personal work showed me how empowering it was to know and take responsibility for my patterns of behaviour, my thoughts and feelings. I learnt to feel and express my feelings in healthy ways, and then to ask, what do I need, and what do I need to do to get it? This sequence interrupted that ingrained tendency to feel stuck, the victim, powerless. I learnt to choose and cultivate life-enhancing habits that would grow new, positive neural pathways. I enjoyed experimenting with different sensory experiences such as massage, perfumes, listening to music and spending time in nature.

At times, I naturally felt exhausted and resentful at the significant financial and personal cost involved in doing this work. I would take long breaks, sometimes several years, to enjoy the new level of awareness I'd reached and to have a respite from the intensity of both personal and professional development. As I edged closer to being my authentic self, I felt lighter, happier and closer to other people. The following quote from *Neurosis and Human Growth* by Karen Horney had a real impact on me: 'As we become free to grow ourselves, we also free ourselves to love and to feel concern for other people.' I so wanted to be a loving, authentic person and I was inspired to continue to keep growing and trusting in myself.

I kept doing the work because I knew there was more; more patterns and limiting beliefs, and more I wanted to know about myself and what potential was waiting in me to be realised. One of the books I read at this time was *Becoming a Person* by Carl R. Rogers, a humanistic psychologist. Rogers believes that we come into the world full of potential and feeling good about ourselves, that within human beings there is a natural motivational force that directs us towards constructive growth and becoming all we can be, but it can be thwarted or blocked by 'conditions of worth' that we experience in childhood. His work affirmed I was on the right path.

Now that the impact of separation from my birthmother had been recognised as a genuine phenomenon, and the subsequent coping mechanisms validated, a natural process of grieving for the loss of her began. Although we had been reunited and had some semblance of an ongoing relationship, it did not fill the void. There was an absence of the loving natural connection and sense of belonging that was lost when we were separated. I realised that I had gone into reunion with my birthmother wounded, needy and hungry for the missed experience of the mother–child bond. These needs, coupled with Sue's own historic pain, for a long time impaired our ability to be together in a safe and loving way. Once I'd gained this insight, I could accept responsibility for my part and let go of unrealistic expectations I had placed on us both.

While being interviewed for this book, Sue revealed that she didn't contact me in the early years of reunion because she had signed away her right when she relinquished me and so she felt I needed to be the one to initiate and to maintain the contact between us. Her revelation took my breath away, as it made sense of her behaviours, and the rollercoaster I felt like I had been on. I had interpreted her lack of contact as a sign that I wasn't important to her, and that was why she had appeared to be disinterested in having a relationship. Relief, followed by sadness and tears, flowed. In that moment, how I wished that we had had this conversation in the early stages of our relationship. The reactivation of the pain of rejection and abandonment had taken a significant toll on our relationship, which could have been avoided if we had had the awareness and the courage to talk about it.

Trust in myself grew as I embraced my pain, sensitivities, patterns and mistakes instead of numbing, burying or flagellating myself for them. Through learning the skill of listening to my heart and intuition, I was able to make conscious choices from my authentic self rather than my ego, personality, conditioned or wounded self. I learnt through the practices of yoga, mindfulness, heart-centred breathing and a growing spiritual life that my defences would soften, and I became more present, and experienced more of who I truly was. I learnt that trust strengthens through being in a relationship with ourselves in a loving and compassionate way.

As the healing work progressed, I felt more self-compassion, and, in time, forgiveness of myself and others naturally flowed from this. This was particularly true of my feelings towards my adoptive mother. When she died and I said my goodbyes, I was in a place where I was able to acknowledge the loss of a healthy mother–daughter connection without blaming either of us. We had both lived with, and never talked in depth about, the legacy of the adoption experience, unconsciously colluding with societal norms not to do so. We paid such a high price as a consequence yet, even today, I'm not sure whether this would be a conversation her generation was equipped to have. The compassion and forgiveness I now felt for us both was incredibly healing. I could fully accept that I had a disability with relationships without feeling bad or flawed.

The next step in my journey towards healing was to take

small risks, step out of my comfort zone and breathe through the fear of rejection, so that I could move closer towards being my authentic self in relationships.

●

Despite feeling exposed, I chose to open up to my friend Debbie, who had held my hand through the highs and lows of my reunion with Sue, and I explained what I now knew and how I had seen it playing out in our own relationship. I cried when she told me she could see this but still loved me, even though my distancing behaviours had caused her pain. She offered her commitment to not allow me to distance myself or to push her away when these feelings were triggered, but to encourage me to have an honest conversation, to tell her how I was feeling. I will be forever grateful to her, as the unconditional love and safety she offered me in our relationship at this time was to change the trajectory of my relationship patterns forever.

I started to enjoy more connection with others, as I was more at ease. I was now awake enough to see that it had been *me* setting myself up for rejection, not others doing it to me; I was primed to see the potential for rejection, then respond as a victim, rather than look for what I wanted and needed. This clarity was incredibly empowering. But it was slow work, it took time and practice, and more pain, as I worked to change this entrenched pattern.

My relationship with Lawrie was the next and closest relationship that needed attention. We had been together since the age of 16. He was my best friend and a supportive partner through the turbulent years of adolescence, reunion with my birth family, the period of intense anxiety, as well as bearing the brunt of my struggle of overcoming adoption-related issues. These, combined with the daily stress of raising and providing for a young family, had taken a toll on him and on our relationship. Our marriage crumbled under the weight of it, and we lived apart for the next nine months.

While separated, we still maintained family outings, and during these times we often found ourselves talking more honestly than we ever had before. We acknowledged the impact of being in a committed relationship at such a young age, and how this had contributed to the challenges; how my sensitivity to abandonment and rejection was hard to deal with, and how his inability to understand and cope with my insecurities made him feel confused and helpless. We acknowledged the toll that adoption-related issues and reunion had taken. We realised that we had not been living together as our true selves and wanted to learn how to do so.

One of the skills we learnt was the practice of owning and communicating our feelings in healthy ways — to be courageous and honest without blaming. We attended several workshops for couples, which supported and rewired new habits. Today, we share an authentic, loving, honest relationship that rarely triggers historic patterns and emotional pain. When we do fall back into old patterns, we recognise it, acknowledge it, work through it and move forward.

Another significant step in the healing process was my involvement with a group of adopted women I met, ranging in age from 35 to 45, who wanted to explore and process their adoption issues in a small-group therapeutic setting. Each of us had been placed for adoption during New Zealand's closed adoption era, and by the time we met, we had all been reunited with our birth families. Despite remarkably diverse backgrounds, adoption experiences, lifestyles and personal circumstances, we were intrigued to find that, collectively, we shared the same core issues, and in sharing our stories, we felt less isolated. The relief at being able to talk openly about adoption in a supportive environment was immense, and being in a group was validating, as it illuminated the very real shared issues resulting from the adoptive experience. We gave and received acceptance and empathy, and created a safe place to learn and develop new ways of being and behaving.

As the group came to a natural close two years later, I realised that I had let go of searching outside myself for love, acceptance and feelings of not belonging, and had let go of being anxious about things I couldn't control. I could see the full spectrum of the adoption experience, not just from my own perspective.

In confronting the myths about adoption, I no longer carried the shame of illegitimacy, but viewed myself as equal to all and worthy of respect. I had matured. It was a delicious place in which to rest and enjoy the fruits of the personal work to date. While I basked in a sense of contentment, I noticed that I felt closer to my adoptive family. I saw that my life was richer and deeper from the experience of having been adopted and I felt grateful.

More days than not I forget that I am adopted, as I feel so

at peace and whole. At times, though, despite the years of personal work, if I am under significant stress, the patterns can return. I know them so well, they are familiar friends, and now I can say, 'Hello, there you are again: abandonment, not good enough, rejection ...' Remembering that only I can sanction these, I breathe slowly and deeply, and allow any feelings to surface without judgement. I ask if they are towards my growth, and if they are true. Occasionally they are, but mostly they are just old fears or pain reappearing for more attention and learning. For example, I would be triggered into an old pattern if Lawrie said he would call and he didn't. Instead of thinking he's had a car accident, or that I'm not important enough, I now think about how things might be for him, and reassure myself that he will be in touch when he is able. It is now not all about me.

There are times when I notice the hyper-vigilant part of me scanning the environment for cues as to how to behave in order to be liked, and to reduce the chance of rejection. Instead of the old pattern of abandoning myself to please others, I acknowledge the pattern, offer kind self-talk that soothes and quiets the anxiety, then use this awareness to move towards people with love and acceptance, and look for the positives in them. I know that no one can reject me without my permission.

Self-knowledge has empowered me to know I need to feel seen, heard and validated, so where appropriate, I ask for this. In the past I would go into a negative spiral if my birthparents didn't contact me. Now, as soon as I notice this, I pick up the phone and call them. In that moment, because I am the one wanting connection, I empower myself by taking responsibility for meeting my needs, and therefore I don't reignite old feelings of isolation or abandonment, nor am I dependent upon others to meet my needs.

My relationship with both my adoptive and birth family is now, I think, as 'normal' as families can be. My relationship with my adoptive father has been one of the closest that I have enjoyed in my life, and since his passing I miss his delightful and loving ways. The memories of his well-lived life and his love for me live on in my heart. It still amazes me that I can now feel love around me and for others, experienced as a *heart-felt* sensation of warmth rather than just my head telling me I am loved but being unable to feel it. My relationship with Sue and Tony has also grown into a mutually nourishing and loving one, for which I am deeply grateful.

●

Both my personal and professional work have brought immense fulfilment and meaning, as well as challenges. It has been a passion and a privilege to work and walk alongside people in their adoption journeys, and naturally, my own enquiry into my experience has informed a deep understanding of other people's journeys.

Traversing the many layers of one's adoptive experience is a courageous and compassionate endeavour. Courageous, because we don't know what we are looking for, what we will find or what we will encounter along the way. When anxiety is activated, it brings up early childhood experiences, trauma residue and stories that are an integral part of what we need to work through and heal. In doing so, we access insights that take us through the barriers to freedom, to grow closer to who we really are. Although it doesn't feel like it at the outset, within each of us is resilience. We are equipped to adapt and survive, we have the strength to face and work through things, as well as the ability to bounce back.

The time I have spent as a counsellor at a hospice talking with people in the last hours and minutes of their lives has taught me that being courageous enough to live a life true to oneself — not the life others expect — and to let ourselves be happier, is the essence of what life is about. In letting go of who and what I thought people wanted me to be, I have fulfilled a deep need to connect and belong.

I want that for you. The most challenging and rewarding part of the journey in waking up and returning home to your authentic self is acknowledging your innate goodness and potential, and saying yes to the life you deserve. Stew Darling, in *Lead Through Life*, writes: 'Ultimately, we are here to love and be loved; most important, in that phase, is our ability to love ourselves.'

Above: Brigitta's birthparents: Jan, skiing in Austria in 1967, and Bob, playing rugby in South Africa in the early 1970s.
Below: Jo's birthparents Sue and Tony, 1958.

PART 3

Severed Ties

CHAPTER 11

I wanted you to have a family
— Jan

The social worker paints the picture. Wealthy, eager 'happily married' adoptive parents who can give the child 'everything' the natural mother can't are queuing up impatiently. If she really loves the baby she can prove it in one way — by handing it over quietly.

— Joss Shawyer, *Death by Adoption*

'What will the neighbours think?' was often the first reaction to news of an unexpected pregnancy in the 1960s. In most cases it was teenagers who found themselves in this position, and they usually felt compelled to share the news with their parents, who invariably ended up making all the decisions about what would happen to the baby. Often a girl would be sent away from home and the whole thing would be hushed up, never to be spoken of again.

My story was different, although the shame and stigma of being unwed and pregnant was still very real. I was 23 when Brigitta was born and I'd just returned from overseas, where, like many New Zealanders, I had gone and done the big OE, living in London and travelling around Europe. Back then, you always went for two years, and then you returned and got on with your life. I had left home and been working since I was 17, but my mother was still worried about how I was going to cope when I left New Zealand. We had always been a very close family and she was rather distressed about my going away, but I loved every minute of it. When my two years were up, I felt I'd pretty much explored all of the countries I wanted to, and I was ready to come home.

What a lot of people don't understand is that back then, many girls like me were brought up with very little freedom. Everyone they mixed with knew their parents, or their brothers or sisters. You were always someone's daughter or someone's sister, never your own person. Because of the personality I had, which was much more subdued than most of my family, I was never 'me', and so that time overseas was about finding out who I was. I became an individual and made my own decisions for the first time in my life.

•

I met Bob aboard the *Northern Star* as it sailed from Southampton to New Zealand in late 1967. The ship was full of Aussies and Kiwis travelling home from their overseas adventures, along with young families from the United

Kingdom starting a new life on the other side of the world. Us young people made the most of the dances, dinners and entertainment offered during the leisurely six-week journey. I got swept up in this fantasy world, where we didn't have to go to work, we didn't have to get up at a certain time. There was no routine to our lives — everything was pleasure. Even though I had been exposed to more liberal attitudes during my years in Europe, I still considered myself a conservative Kiwi girl, bound by the conventions and values of my upbringing. I'd had a few relationships in the past, but nothing serious.

Bob boarded the boat in Durban. He was Australian but had been working in South Africa for a few years and was going back home to visit his parents. He was about seven years older than me. The relationship developed very quickly. They talked about 'shipboard romances' back then, and everyone knew about them, but even though my brain might have said 'don't get involved', my emotions were not as sensible. Also, we were together all the time on the boat, so it was much more intense.

I fell in love. We talked about an ongoing relationship. I really thought that although he was getting off in Sydney, we would correspond, and he would come over to New Zealand or I would go over to Australia. I believed there was a future. I got the impression he hadn't been home for the whole time he'd been based in South Africa. In those days, the only affordable way to travel long distances was by boat, so it wasn't just a case of hopping on a plane to visit your parents back home. The relationship developed, but I still considered myself a 'good' girl. I did know better than to get seriously involved, so I tried to stop any physical relationship from developing. We only had sex the one time — the night before he got off the boat — and the next morning we were waiting for the ship to dock and I walked down the gangplank and felt a 'click'. I remember it so distinctly and I believe that was the moment I became pregnant. I've always remembered it. It was a powerful feeling, but of course I put it to one side and never thought any more about it.

I carried on to New Zealand and went home to where my parents were farming. I stayed with them for a couple of months and it was while I was there that I realised I might be pregnant. I went to a doctor in town — not our usual family doctor — and he confirmed it. It was such a shock that I could get pregnant so easily. I was just so innocent about those kinds of things. Bob and I had been corresponding all that time. We used to write every four or five days, so I wrote immediately and told him. I presumed he would ring or write straight back to say that he'd be over as soon as possible. That was what I expected to happen. There was no panic involved. I just thought, well this is the way it is, and we'll figure it out together. It wasn't a disaster in my mind. I really thought, from the letters we wrote, that we would be together. We hadn't finalised any plans, but I was in no hurry. I was enjoying spending some time with my family and I wanted to take things as they came.

Bob's letter in response to my news said that he was sorry about the situation I was in and when it was all over, he hoped we might be able to get together again. I was devastated. It was really the first and only time that I was shocked and upset because I realised it was now all up to me. I felt like he'd let me down, and I didn't want anything more to do with him, so I wrote back saying maybe we'd been lucky in some way because I'd had a miscarriage and I was going to get on with my life on my own. By now I was worried that some time in the future he might just show up and feel he had a right to be involved in decisions about the child. I didn't want to be tied to someone who wasn't there to support me when I needed him. I wished him a happy life and said I didn't want to hear from him again. And I never did.

I knew I wasn't going to tell my parents. Not long before I returned home, they had taken on a returned services farm, and they had absolutely no money. My mother had brought up five children, plus she had partially raised several nephews. Almost all the children in the neighbourhood had at some stage lived with my parents because mum was a wonderful mother, very loving and she was excellent with young children, but I felt that she had done her dash. She was tired. The only way I could see it working, if I told them, was that they would bring the child up, and I didn't want that. As lovely as she was, my mother could also be a bit of a snob, and she would have been mortified by what the neighbours thought. I felt they had enough burdens with the farm and my siblings — especially my youngest sister whom they were terribly upset with at the time; they didn't need my problems as well.

I'd got myself into this situation and it was up to me to deal with it, but I knew that whatever happened, deciding what would be best for my child was the most important decision of my life. I couldn't live with myself if I let my parents or anyone else make it for me. If I was going to survive this, I had to make up my own mind.

While I was overseas, I'd met a friend who had asked me to be her bridesmaid, so in about February (I'd arrived back in December) I went down to where she lived in the South Island and stayed with her parents. It was great timing because after the wedding, her parents asked me to stay on. They had a farm and employed labourers, and I helped her mother with the cooking and cleaning. It gave me time to decide what I was going to do. I wrote to my parents and said I loved it down south and wanted to go and live in Christchurch.

That removed me from the home environment so I didn't have to explain morning sickness or anything like that to my parents. It allowed me time to find a flat in Christchurch and I joined a temping agency, where I managed to keep working until about June. Nobody knew I was pregnant, although I suspect my friend's mother might have guessed. I'd had morning sickness while I was staying there, but I'd explained to her that I often got migraines and had bilious attacks as a result. I don't know whether she believed me or not, but nothing was ever said. I didn't tell my friend and I saw her after I'd had the baby, but she never made any comment. I was very fit in those days as I walked a lot, and I was slim, so nobody ever suspected anything because I don't think I showed particularly. Clothes were quite loose back then anyway.

When I saw a doctor in Christchurch, he asked me what I was going to do. I told him that I was going to have the child adopted but didn't want to stay in Christchurch, so he gave me the phone numbers and addresses of some places in

Dunedin and Invercargill. I had already decided that I wanted to go to a Salvation Army home. During the war my father had had dealings with the Salvation Army, and he talked about them with so much love and respect for the work they had done that it had a positive association for me, plus I'd seen advertisements for them and knew they were non-judgemental. That mattered to me.

Abortion was never a consideration. Nobody suggested it. I knew about it, but it was just something I would never have done. In all the years after I gave my baby up, I realised that if I were ever in that situation again, I still wouldn't have been able to go through with an abortion. I believe that every woman has that right, but I also believe that every woman has to do what is right for her at the time. For me it wasn't right.

My way of finding out about things has always been to read, and that's what I did. I got hold of several books on adoption as well as some pamphlets from the doctor. They reinforced what we were told back then: adoption was a positive thing to do and the best way to treat children born out of wedlock; we were doing our child a disservice if they weren't adopted; the 'selfless' thing was to give them two parents and a loving family.

I kept in contact with my parents, but in those days we only wrote letters, we didn't ring, so they had no opportunity to pick up from my voice that anything might be wrong. When I went to the Salvation Army home in Dunedin, I couldn't have my parents writing to me there so I applied for a post office box. I said I was working as a nanny for a family with young children, and they sent my letters to the post office. Because I walked everywhere, I managed to clear the box every few days and kept up a correspondence without them getting suspicious. Of course, they knew about Bob because I'd been getting lots of letters from him when I first came back, but I just said we'd broken up. They'd never met him, so they didn't expect anything else.

The only time I ever had a problem with my family while I was pregnant was when my mother wrote to ask if my sister could come and stay with me in Dunedin for her holiday. I had to write back and say it wasn't possible because the lady I was working for was sick, and I was in charge of her two children while her husband was away. I got quite good at thinking on my feet.

•

I was making my own decisions and I remember feeling in control, not really distressed about anything. The home in Dunedin in 1968 was fantastic — well, to me it was. I got on very well with the matron, and possibly because I was older, she would talk to me. In the mornings we did domestic work — the laundry, dishes, cooking and so on — to help with the running of the home, then in the afternoons we were free. Most of the girls, particularly the young ones, would read or just sit around and chat, but I never really got close to the other girls, again possibly because I was older.

The matron seemed to realise I was different from the others as she talked to me a lot about adoption and shared stories about the families that took the children in. Some of them would come back and visit her, so that helped me to feel comfortable about the process. I did get upset at times.

I remember standing in a doorway in Dunedin waiting for the bus to come. The home was on top of one of the hills and towards the end of my pregnancy when I was tired, I would sometimes catch the bus. I have this memory of standing there feeling sad about everything. It was August, in the depths of a southern winter, raining and miserable. I never felt like I was going to change my mind though.

We were encouraged to give our baby a name. I wanted something that I wasn't going to hear again, even though I knew that the adoptive families never kept the original name. I chose the name 'Brigitta'. I had read a book about a woman from Egypt with this name and I liked it. Then when she was born, I felt it suited her.

The first three or four days were very hard. You do a lot of crying anyway, even mothers who have husbands and other children. We weren't allowed to go to the nursery, but the babies were brought out to us and we could feed and play with them, and have that time together. I tried to block out of my mind that I was going to give her up. I focused on enjoying the time I had, although there were times where I just couldn't stop the tears. You know you have to make this decision, yet it never feels like it's the right decision. It's not the one you ever thought you were going to have to make.

I had her with me for 10 days. I was able to give her a bottle, play with her and get to know her a little bit. I'd think 'I can't do this', and then, 'What are my options?' There were other girls who changed their minds. I remember one girl I became friendly with after Brigitta was born. She was Australian and had come over to have her baby. She was very close to taking her little boy back with her, but in the end, she just couldn't do it. Everyone around you is going through the same dilemma, while the staff are encouraging you that you're doing the right thing. You can't think about yourself; you've got to think of your baby. Their future and what sort of life they're going to have depends on you giving them up.

Eventually I started to feel stronger and say to myself, 'Well, I've made this decision, so I've got to stick with it.' Once the solicitor came, I was told there was no chance to change my mind — this was the last opportunity. He did say, 'Now, are you sure about this?' and I just said 'Yes' and signed the papers. I think the matron said I had six months before it was final, but I knew I could never take a child away from the adoptive parents. I was never ever going to do that to another family. What would it do to a child to go from you, to other parents, and then be taken away again?

I didn't see anyone from social welfare during the process. I think I saw the solicitor a couple of days beforehand, or maybe even the day before, to sign the papers. It was the matron who asked me what I wanted for my child and wrote down all the information. I said it was important that she have a good education, that she have the opportunity if she wanted to go to university, and that I'd prefer she be in a family with other children rather than be an only child because I had been brought up with brothers and sisters. Really, those were the only things. I didn't specify religion or an ethnic group or anything else.

When they found a family for Brigitta, they told me that she would have two older brothers and that her father was an engineer. This encouraged me; if he had gone to university, perhaps they'd be agreeable to my child being well educated. I did feel she had gone to a good family, but I just felt numb. The small amount of information I was given didn't really convince me I had done the right thing, but I had to keep telling myself, 'Forget about me and think about what's best for Brigitta.' And there were no other options. If someone had come and said, 'Look, we're prepared to find you a house where you can live with others, you can have a job and there will be childcare for your child,' that would have given me an option I could have taken. I suppose even at that late stage I could have told my parents and waited to see what they thought, but this was about me and about deciding what I thought was going to be right for my baby. Even if my parents had offered to bring Brigitta up, I knew in my heart that wasn't ideal; I wanted her to have a family, and I didn't believe I could give her that.

She was a very relaxed baby. She didn't cry. I can still visualise her on the bed, and I'd take all the wrappings off and play with her hands. She'd just be kicking away, and other babies would be crying, but she'd be lying there quite happy, with her dark hair. She was sleepy because she had a bit of jaundice, but she fed relatively well. My pregnancy was not really a traumatic time for either of us; we just got through it.

The worst day was the last one, of course. That last feed — it was very hard. A lot of girls chose not to do that last feed on the tenth day, but I chose to because I wanted to say goodbye. It was something I needed to do. So, I gave her the bottle and then I didn't play with her, I just held her against me. The nurse came ... and she just took her away.

You have to do some hard things in your life.

CHAPTER 12

The family that never was
— Sue and Tony

> The uniting truth about adoption is the fact that it always involves loss.
>
> — Julie Jarrell Bailey, *The Adoption Reunion Survival Guide*

Sue

I was working at my first job in an accountant's office in the late 1950s when I met Tony, Jo's father. I lived at Days Bay, just out of Wellington, with Mum, my sister and two brothers. My parents were divorced, and things hadn't been easy for my mother, but I had great friends from my school days and was enjoying life.

I was quite religious when I was young and enjoyed going to Sunday School, then later to Bible class, and my best friend at the time was a minister's daughter. I loved the feeling that I was part of something. I met Tony at a youth-club dance and we started 'going steady'. I fell completely in love with him, and in time our passion reached its inevitable conclusion, but I was so naive, I had no idea I could get pregnant. There was no discussion about contraception — we just got carried away in the moment.

I used to catch the bus to work with Mum. She was working in an insurance office, so we would go into the city together each day. I remember getting off the bus at Days Bay and being violently ill in front of her. Although Mum had had four children, she wasn't what would be called a 'woman of the world'; maybe deep down she suspected that I was pregnant, but she didn't say anything, and I hadn't even given it a thought. After three months or so, I knew something was wrong. I kept hoping my period would come and when it didn't, I eventually asked a girlfriend for the name of a doctor. I took myself off to this female doctor and she was just awful — an older woman with absolutely no heart. Looking back, she was quite cruel. She examined me and said, 'You're pregnant.'

Naturally, I burst into tears and said, 'What am I going to do?' I was so ashamed that I had let my mother down after all she had been through. The doctor told me she could send me to a farm in Taihape, a small community several hours' drive from Wellington, so I agreed, the phone call was made and it was organised on the spot. I went home and told Mum that I was pregnant but she didn't need to worry because I was going away to have the baby. There was no question of me keeping it at such a young age. I can't remember her reaction, but I know I had her support, which was amazing as there was such shame attached to unmarried mothers in those days.

Mum arranged for me to be taken to Taihape by a friend who

was a commercial traveller. I don't know what she told him, nor can I remember what story we made up for my brothers and sister, but I think we said I had a job looking after children up north.

The farming couple in Taihape had five children. I was their servant, really, and my days were consumed with housework, scrubbing floors, preparing meals, washing and ironing. My only sanctuary was my little room at the back of the house. Tony came up a couple of times, plus my mum and Tony's mother. They were my only visitors. There were no phone calls or emails, of course, very little contact with anyone, so it was a lonely time.

I had no idea what adoption really meant. Nobody I knew had ever been through one and I just blanked everything out and went along with it. The authorities I dealt with, such as the doctor I first visited and the medical staff at the hospital, were brutal. There was neither sympathy nor understanding — I got pushed from one person to the next and did what I was told to do.

The birth was excruciating. I remember the farmer's wife driving me to the hospital in the middle of the night. She threw me into the jeep with a face cloth to bite on. It was the bumpiest road — no tar-seal or anything. She was a very masculine woman and I remember her driving flat out, swearing and cursing about men. I don't remember much more other than coming to and being cut and stitched. My baby was taken away from me straight away. There was no kindness or caring. I was treated like a leper. As far as the adoption process went, I guess I just filled out the forms. I did ask for my baby to go to a religious family because I thought they would ensure a better quality of life. I must have known it was a girl because I named her Shirley after my mother. I understood I would never see her again and there was no emotional support given at all.

After it was over, I went back to the farm for a short time, then the same neighbour who had driven me up took me back to Wellington. I had obviously put on weight and was so terrified that people would know what had happened, but in those days people didn't speak out like they do today, and nobody ever asked me where I had been. I found out many years later that some of my old school friends had suspected something, but it was just what happened: girls disappeared for months at a time and when they came back, they simply got on with their lives.

By the time I returned to the city, Tony had gone farming and I was devastated to find him gone. I'm sure he was pushed into it — I think his mother organised for him to go in order to get him out of Wellington. I always felt she didn't believe I was good enough for her son. I got a job as soon as I could, and also took on a second job cleaning at night to save money to go to Sydney with my best friend. I was so lucky that she was planning to go when she was as it enabled me to get away. I wanted to escape the guilt and shame of my secret.

I didn't tell anyone what had happened for many years. I had lost not only my child but also the person I had been in love with. This experience made me afraid to get close to people. I didn't make attachments. I buried the past as deeply as I could, and I blocked out my feelings. Once I moved to Sydney, I felt fortunate that my friends who were having babies were still living in New Zealand so I wasn't subjected to seeing babies and happy families around me, to be reminded of what I'd lost.

Obviously, I thought of my baby often and her birthday was the saddest day. I hoped and prayed that she was being loved and cared for, and that she was happy.

Tony

I'll never forget Sue ringing me up at work to tell me she was pregnant. We'd been going out for quite a while at that stage, but she called me up one day out of the blue. The guy who answered the phone didn't hang up straight away when I took the call and she just blurted out, 'Tony, Tony, I've been to the doctor and I'm pregnant.' The other bloke quickly put the phone down and never said anything to me about it. Sue was in such a state. It was just a total shock.

My first thought was, 'God, get me out of here!' As a male, I think you just don't want to have to deal with it; you want to escape. Socially, in the 1950s, sex before marriage wasn't acceptable, even though it was going on like crazy, of course. No one was allowed to talk about it and there was no contraception available, so, when pregnancies happened, in most cases people simply got married. That was the usual expectation.

I was only 17 and Sue was 16 when we met. We didn't think about the consequences of having sex — it was purely a pleasurable thing and it never crossed our minds that it could result in a child. We were young and we were physical. We liked doing lots of different things together and had a lot of fun. We both loved dancing and Sue was a great dancer. It was the rock and roll era and we used to meet at the Karori Youth Club every weekend.

I don't remember telling my mother about Sue being pregnant, but she certainly got involved at some point. She ran the household and decided she was going to have a say in any arrangements that were made. She didn't tell my father, or my brother and sister. She felt Sue and I were from very different backgrounds and she thought we'd struggle to maintain a long-term relationship, and that's why we didn't get married.

Sue and I saw each other for a little while after we found out she was pregnant, but then she was shipped off to Taihape. There were families back then that used pregnant women as household help and to look after kids. Because it was such a common thing in those days for young girls to get pregnant outside of marriage, there was a whole system set up to accommodate them, especially with no single-mother benefits. We lived in a very small community just out of Wellington and everybody knew everybody. No one who I knew had been through a similar experience; certainly none of my mates had got a girl pregnant. There were only two options: marriage or adoption.

Once Sue went away, I did go up to visit her a couple of times. Mum remained involved and I remember her making some winter pregnancy dresses for Sue. Then the baby was born, but I don't remember being told anything about it — what sex it was or any details. The only thing I did know was that a minister's family adopted the baby. Everyone thought that was great; it meant the child had gone to a respectable family and a good home. Of course, in those days it wasn't an open adoption, so you had no access to any information about the child, and there was no suggestion of any interaction afterwards. It was just locked up. Sue eventually came back to Wellington and then she went off to Australia.

    I put it behind me and got on with my life.

Above: Jo and family (from left): Hollie, Hugo, Evie, Jo, Jack and Will, on holiday in Australia in 2020.

Below: Brigitta and family (from left): Jade, Andrew, Brigitta and Zoë.

PART 4

The Legacy

CHAPTER 13

The ripple effect

> For adoptees, the need to defend against the possibility of abandonment or other losses intrudes into almost every relationship, beginning with that of the adoptive mother and including their relationships to friends, lovers, and even themselves.
>
> — Nancy Newton Verrier, *The Primal Wound*

What are the repercussions of adoption and reunion on those who share their lives with adopted people? Realistically, you can't expect to separate a mother from her child at birth without creating some sort of legacy.

Through these stories written from those closest to us, our birthparents, partners and children, we uncover some of the hidden wounds of relinquishment that we carried into future relationships, and share what played out following reunion with our birth families.

Jan

After Brigitta went to her new family, I must have stayed at the home for another week or so, and helped out in the nursery. Lots of girls didn't want to have anything to do with their baby once it was born, so I was able to help with feeding, bathing and looking after the babies. That was how I coped, that was why I survived. From there I went and trained as a Karitane nurse in Dunedin, and for the next five years all the love and affection I would have given to Brigitta went into other children.

Newborn babies were brought into the Karitane hospitals often because there was something wrong. Sometimes they hadn't bonded with their mother, they might have an illness, or sometimes it was the young mothers who couldn't cope. I think becoming a Karitane nurse was really the only thing that got me through. If I'd done anything else, I don't know what would have happened to me. All that maternal instinct was channelled, and I was particularly good with small babies — I really had an empathy with them. I could help them and their mothers and it gave me a purpose. Perhaps my experience hadn't been wasted because now I was helping others.

Over the years I was always worried that if something had happened to Brigitta, such as her being put back into social welfare care, I wouldn't be told. I could cope with her going to a loving family, but if her circumstances changed and she wasn't with that family any more, then I knew I wouldn't be consulted, and I felt torn that I had no rights. It was the not knowing that ate away at me over the years — not even knowing if she was alive.

The worst time was definitely from straight after Brigitta was born until she was five. I remember being in Dunedin at the time she turned five, when she would have just started school, and me sitting outside the schools to see if I could recognise her. I always presumed she had stayed in Dunedin and I had this urge to try to find her. I don't know why age five was any more significant, but I guess it was a benchmark. I thought if I went to all the primary schools in Dunedin and watched the little ones come out at two o'clock before the older children, I might just see her. I would never have done anything; I had made a bargain and committed myself to not being part of her life. It had been my promise to her parents, in my mind, that this was their child. I just wanted to watch and see if I could spot her. All I wanted was reassurance that she was still alive, that she looked all right, and that someone was meeting her after school.

Realistically, I knew I never would see her, and I wouldn't have recognised her anyway, but it was just something I had to do. When I saw children in the park, I would think about her and say to myself, 'Well, she'd be that age now and this is what she'd be doing.' I've always done that. The only person I told in all those years was one boyfriend, and after that I never saw him again — he just didn't know how to deal with it.

After I finished my training in the Karitane hospital, I went and lived in people's homes caring for children. I didn't enjoy that as much because you are literally living other people's lives, so then I moved to the Hawke's Bay Fallen Soldiers' Memorial Hospital and worked in the newborn unit, and I absolutely loved it. But as time passed, the rules changed, and I needed to be a registered nurse to do that type of work. By then, I was ready for a change too; I felt I'd worked it out of my system. My baby would have been 10 years old by then — not a baby any longer.

I had made a conscious decision not to have any more children of my own. I had lost a child, and I wasn't going to put myself in a position of vulnerability again, nor could I visualise having another child. I think my caring for children after Brigitta was born took out of me all the maternal instincts I had. I just gave and gave and gave, to the point where that longing for children was not there. Then, when I got married, I took on two stepsons whom I focused my love and attention on.

August was always a bad month. I was never without the loss — it was always there. Right up until Brigitta was in her twenties, I would feel odd for a few days before her birthday. I didn't always connect it with her, but I would just feel a little bit down. Then I would realise that it was the twenty-fourth, the day she was born. The feelings would last for about a week over the time of her birthday: I'd be a little quieter, a little down, and need to just go off by myself and walk. Not consciously thinking about what might have been or anything like that, just acknowledging it. I couldn't let my mind wander too much, I just had to keep going. Maybe I should have had a ritual for that date, something I could look forward to rather than it being a time of sadness and grieving, but each year at that time I needed to grieve. In a way it's a death and as far as I was concerned, I was never going to see her again.

One of the things that surprised me tremendously when I heard from Brigitta was that her parents had kept the name I gave her. I chose a name I thought I would never hear again, and I did hear the name only once in all the years before we were reunited. I was with my cousin and she said she was just going up to see a friend called Brigitta. I froze. Of course, I quickly realised that her friend would be a lot older than my Brigitta, but at the time it was a huge shock. I was so sure that her parents would change her name because it was so unusual, difficult to spell and difficult to say. I never thought of naming her after anyone in my family or after anyone I knew. She was an individual who needed a name that was hers. That was her 10-day name — I didn't know it was going to be hers forever.

When I heard that it was still her name, I thought she must have had very special parents because the usual thing was to change it; to wipe out anything that had gone before. It was also out of respect to them and for what they had done that I never said that the way it was spelt and pronounced wasn't quite the way I had chosen. I got a shock when Andrew first said her name to me over the phone, but I decided not to say anything. I didn't feel I had any right to correct it so I went along with what they had used for all those years.

I think Brigitta found it hard that I never tried to find her, despite me always hoping she was happy and well-cared for. I told her that I never would have because I gave her to another family. I had no right to go and disrupt her life. What I'd done to her was bad enough and I certainly wasn't going to make her life any worse by showing up out of the blue. I did feel, deep down, that I'd done something bad, despite everyone telling me I had done the right thing. I always thought Brigitta might be resentful of the fact that I had done this. Maybe that was all part of my fear of trying to find her. Probably it's still a fear I have.

After we were reunited, I waited for her to turn around and tell me that I should not have done it, but the first thing Brigitta said to me was that I did the right thing in giving her to her adoptive parents. She's never blamed me for what's happened in her life, and that's why we have a good relationship now. I feel that the family who raised her has helped make her who she is today. She's a lovely woman; she's kind and considerate. She's broadminded — and that's come from her adoptive parents. It would have been different if I'd brought her up, but it might not have been better.

I owe Brigitta's parents a huge debt that I can never repay. If I'd known what had happened to Brigitta through those 40 years, I think I would have been more at peace with myself, more accepting of other people instead of always putting up a wall. And perhaps it would have freed me up to think some more about myself, instead of always placing other people first. But I feel that if I had searched, it might not have been what Brigitta wanted. It might have disrupted her life, and what right did I have to do that to her? I don't think I ever allowed myself to think that she might have wanted me to find her.

I followed the law change in 1985 word for word. It did cross my mind then that Brigitta might search for me. It was in the newspapers and on television, so there was no way I could have missed it. They explained everything you needed to know about putting a block on the information if you didn't want to have contact. But if she needed to find me, I wasn't going to deny her.

●

When Brigitta first made contact, I hadn't told my husband about her, and I'd never told my parents. My husband was recently separated and we were both mature people when we met and we'd agreed that there were certain aspects of our past that we wouldn't share. I had no desire to risk sharing that part of my life with anyone again.

I used to hear stories of reunion through the years, but for every good story there was a negative one. I have a cousin who found her birthmother but she just shut the door in her face. Always in my mind was the thought that I didn't want to upset Brigitta. She could have been horrified if I had just shown up. Sometimes I would imagine going into a social welfare office and making some enquiries about what to do. If Brigitta had tried to trace me, I had always presumed that she would do it through social welfare and perhaps there would be a letter first to tell me that she was searching. It was such a huge shock hearing Andrew, Brigitta's husband, on the phone when they first made contact.

Another fear was that if I did contact her, she might be disappointed. Not in terms of what I was like, exactly, but just that fear of rejection. If I got in touch with her and she slammed the door in my face, how would I cope with that? That was a lesser concern, though; my main barrier to searching for her was that I didn't want to disturb the happy life I hoped she was having.

It was during the period when Brigitta was between 16 and 20 that I thought quite seriously about what I would do if I received a letter from social welfare. Each year that passed I would think, 'Well, it hasn't happened, she hasn't made contact yet.' Then I remember vague thoughts later on such as, 'She's a mature adult now with her own family. Her children will just about be grown up. It's not going to happen; she's not going to make contact.'

My parents were still alive at that point, so there was some degree of relief that I would never have to tell them about Brigitta. That would have been a hurdle. Up until then, if she had made contact, I knew I would meet up in such a way that nobody else had to know. I never visualised anything more than one meeting, having a cup of coffee and talking. After that, if there was further contact, it might be once every five years. I never envisaged a relationship or being part of her family — she'd have a relationship with her own family, there wouldn't be room for me.

For a long time after she made contact, it was very hard to relax into it. I thought we'd get to the stage where we would think enough is enough and we'd withdraw. But that has never happened, and that's because of Brigitta. Especially in the early stages, she pushed it forward and wouldn't let me drop back. It did get hard sometimes and I felt like I was struggling to cope, but because of the way she managed the relationship, it was okay. I held back a bit because for a long time I was waiting for the recriminations from Brigitta, thinking each time we met that this might be when she brings it up. It was what I was expecting, and I knew I was going to be really hurt. I would have understood why she felt that way, but there was such a fear about when it would happen.

For probably the first year I was expecting her to call it quits at any time. I coped with that by just taking things one step at a time. I'd think, at least I can be grateful I've met her; I know what her children look like, and what her life is like. That's more than I had known before. I would have accepted knowing only those little pieces. But any amount, I was grateful for, and I still feel that way. If she decides at any point that she wants to go on with her life without me, I will accept that. I would be very upset if I didn't have an ongoing relationship with her, but if she ever doesn't want to continue, I hope there is enough of a link now with her girls that they would remember me and get in touch in the future.

I suspect there will always be some anxiety in me about the relationship because of the way I am. It's nothing to do with how Brigitta treats me; it is about me as a person. In a way, I almost can't believe that good things can happen to me. I don't really have any reason to feel that way because I had a happy and stable upbringing, but my mother was like this, too. It was made worse by giving Brigitta up. I put the blame on myself and didn't think I deserved much in life and that what I'd done was wrong. I still feel guilty, even seeing how well things have turned out for her. I don't think that will ever change. It's only more recently through the reading I have done that I understand the damages inflicted on a child by taking it from its mother. I really did believe at the time that I was making the right choice for Brigitta. It's only recently after all these years that I've started having doubts.

Meeting Brigitta has shown me all the love I've missed out on. That's the part that is hard to cope with. I don't dwell on it; I try to put it out of my mind. I've been self-contained for a long time. The feelings are so locked away that I don't believe anything would ever allow them to be released or change how I feel. You can't get those years back, but I know I've lost something.

The other relationships around me became challenging once we were reunited. I have always been aware that I never wanted Brigitta's adoptive mother to be hurt, and if I felt that was happening, I would have stepped back — not completely — but it's important to me that she feels she is Brigitta's mother and that she is above me in importance in Brigitta's life. I'm grateful that there were people out there like Brigitta's parents who wanted the children that their mothers couldn't keep.

Having said that, in my heart I do feel like I am Brigitta's mother, and the more time that goes past, the more strongly I feel that. I talk about 'my daughter' and I feel really comfortable and good saying that in front of people who don't know the situation. It has taken some time to reach that stage and to feel natural about saying it.

My husband initially coped very well, although he found the fact that I hadn't told him about her hard to deal with. There was also a sense of sadness that we hadn't had a child together, but we can't change that. We can't go back. Having Brigitta become part of our lives has changed the family dynamic, and that is difficult to juggle. I feel like I want to be with my daughter and her family all the time because I feel so comfortable and welcome, but I also have to balance this with the needs of my husband. Sometimes I feel as if I am split in two.

As much as reunion is about the child you gave up, it is also about the family you already have. That is what makes it so challenging, but for me, looking at what I have gained from having Brigitta and her family in my life, it has been worth it.

Sue

I married a number of years after I had given birth to Jo and I told my husband very early on that I'd had a child out of wedlock, which he accepted. We did try for a family after we got married, but nothing happened, month after month, so we just accepted it. I wasn't devastated about it — we just felt it was one of those things. We had friends who didn't have children, and our lives revolved around other interests.

I kept the experience locked away for 20 years, and then out of the blue I received a letter from Tony's mother to say that she had traced Jo through Jigsaw. The shock was immense. She wanted me to meet Jo, but I just couldn't do it; I couldn't face the emotions. I was at work when I got the letter and I reacted like an ostrich; I put my head in the sand and didn't want to know anything about it. I think Tony came over to Sydney to try to convince me to change my mind. There was absolutely no way. It was gone and buried as far as I was concerned, and I wanted to leave it there. But, through Tony's perseverance, the meeting did come about. He simply hounded me and wore me down — that's the only reason I got on the plane to New Zealand.

Meeting Jo was very emotional. I had a strong sense of trepidation. Tony picked me up at the airport, which was traumatic in itself, and he took me to a motel. There was a wretched maid in the room when we arrived, right at the crucial moment, so Tony had to ask her to leave. Jo was standing on the balcony with her back to me as we walked through the door. She turned and we just ran into each other's arms. It was overwhelming. We were like two magnets drawing together. Although I felt I had been bullied into meeting her, it was all meant to be — it felt so right. I don't think I have ever cried so much in my life — tears of such regret and sadness, tears for Jo being abandoned, tears for letting my mother down, tears for my losses. They just kept coming.

After that, the rest of the weekend was a blank. I remember the connection I felt with Jo, but I was completely overwhelmed. I couldn't cope with it all. I'm quite a sensitive person anyway and the whole situation made me feel like I was, from my toenails up, bubbling over with the intensity of it. I can't think of many other experiences where I haven't been able to call on some sort of coping skills, but in this case, it was all too much.

I got on a plane back to Australia the next morning without seeing Jo again.

After that first meeting, I really let Jo drive things. It wasn't easy to have a relationship with me based in Australia and her in New Zealand, but I did feel that we would continue to be a part of each other's lives. I left that up to Jo. I wasn't going to say, 'Well, I've found her and I'm her mother now,' or anything like that. I didn't think I had a right to be a mother to her because I hadn't been in her life for 21 years. I hadn't earned it. Neither am I the sort of person who would impose or push for anything. It's not my personality. I felt my role in Jo's life was just to be her birthmother, whatever she wanted that to mean. I'm her birthmother, but I don't believe I deserve the title of mother.

The hardest part about meeting Jo and having her come back into my life was telling people about her because I'd kept it a secret for so long, but once I got over the trauma of explaining to friends and family about what had happened in my past, it was fine. They accepted it because they love me and everyone was thrilled, so there were no problems. I've been very lucky.

My husband of course knew that I'd had a child and he just adored Jo when he met her. They got on well and we both liked Lawrie a lot, so it was all very comfortable. The whole family was very positive about the situation. Jo and Lawrie came and lived with us in Sydney for a while, and before that we'd got to know each other through phone calls and letters. I liked Jo's adoptive parents, although her adoptive mother was totally different from my mother and me. I remember when we met them, Mum said how wonderful it all was, and I recall Jo's adoptive mother saying there was enough love for us all. I thought, 'How lovely is that?' It was a very generous thing to say, but I could see how difficult it must have been for Jo to be raised by her. It seemed like a real mismatch, which was very sad to see because I'd had such a wonderful relationship with my mum and Jo has missed out on that. I really felt for her.

My relationship with Jo is not something I feel I've had to work at or consciously think about too much. The relationship is just in my heart. I can't really explain it. Nor is there a formula for success in having a relationship with a child who was adopted. It is completely dependent on the personalities involved and the circumstances. I have had friends who have had a terrible time when they have been reunited with their children — there are some unhappy stories out there — but Jo and I have been able to connect, and I think that is the key.

Tony

Jo has asked me if I thought about her through the years, on her birthday and other times, but I don't think guys are like that. I certainly wasn't, anyway. After she was born it was another 20 years before I really thought about her again, and that was when, without any warning, Mum came and told me she had found Jo. It was a complete shock.

I knew that Mum worked for Jigsaw, but I didn't make the connection that it had anything to do with her trying to find her grand-daughter. I thought she was just doing a good deed and had got involved in something useful. To hear that she had tracked Jo down and now wanted me to meet her was completely unexpected. I think she was driven by guilt to find Jo; she had played a major role in her being adopted by discouraging me from marrying Sue, and I felt this might have been her way of trying to make amends.

Personally, it was terrible timing because I was going through a rough period in my marriage and had three young children. I had never told my wife about having another child, even though I'd thought about it at times during the marriage, but I was a coward. That was a mistake because not telling my wife about Jo proved to be the final straw for her. I was now confronted with a situation I'd had no choice in. Mum had made all the arrangements and there was no question about whether I wanted to be involved. I was railroaded into it and felt the same way as I had at 17: that I simply had to go along with what had been decided.

I can't remember the timespan between Mum telling me about Jo and the meeting taking place, but I was working part-time in Sydney, so I arranged to meet up with Sue to discuss Jo coming on the scene. She and I hadn't been in contact for 20 years but, again, Mum had taken over and had already written to tell her about Jo. I guess I met up with Sue because she was reluctant to get involved and I believed she needed to be persuaded. When I found out she hadn't had any other children of her own, I thought she would be receptive to the idea of meeting Jo, but obviously it was such a deeply ingrained hurt that she just didn't want to deal with it. She had been living in Sydney for a long time; she had her own life and friends who knew nothing about this part of her past. I felt I really had to talk her around, while I recognised that, for Jo, meeting us was important. I probably also felt that Sue needed to finally face it and deal with it.

In terms of the arrangements for the actual meeting, I know it all seemed to come around quite quickly. I have a very clear mental picture of Jo and Lawrie walking up my driveway, but it's hard to remember how I felt about it all. It was quite a difficult thing for me to do on my own, with Sue not there at that stage. I do remember an overwhelming sense of guilt. We had abandoned this child and now here she was fully grown. Combined with the issues I was going through in my marriage, it was all really stressful and overwhelming.

I didn't have a sense that Jo looked like my other children when I first met her — although it was difficult to tell because they were much younger — but there wasn't a feeling of recognition initially. I remember there was a period where I questioned the authenticity of the experience. I'd never met this person before, and I tried to find a commonality. Are there common character traits, looks and personality? There is a credibility issue to start with. It's not like being in a shop where everything has a label on it. My first reaction was, 'Can this be true? My mother has put us together, but did she get it right?' Perhaps because of this I held back a bit, although it didn't feel like it was a difficult process. It was awkward, but not difficult, because Jo and Lawrie were decent people. They were a nice 'package' and didn't come with lots of horrible baggage.

•

The moment you meet your child they become real and it is quite different to thinking about a nameless, faceless entity. You're meeting them for the first time, but there is already a bond there. I think Jo and I really connected, and that day was the beginning of her becoming part of our family. Introducing her to the rest of the family wasn't easy, though. With my other children being quite young, it was a shock to them and perhaps they felt a bit of competition with an older sibling coming onto the scene. My eldest son, in particular, felt displaced, I think, whereas the other two accepted Jo pretty quickly.

Telling my wife about Jo was extremely awkward and all I could do was be upfront and deal with the consequences. I wished I'd been honest about it at the start of our relationship, but back in those days, the chances of a reunion and your child suddenly showing up on your doorstep were almost non-existent. My wife and her parents seemed to think I had done something underhand by not revealing this part of my past before we got married, but I honestly felt it was something I had put behind me.

Jo and I then just progressed along, with the focus more on the development of Sue's involvement with Jo. It took a lot of effort to get her involved, and even though I didn't think it was really my responsibility to facilitate it, I still felt it was the right thing to do. Jo used to get very distressed about the situation with Sue and I felt I could support her through that — and she and I connected through this process.

The only difficult aspect I had with Jo was her attitude over me being with her children. In fact, at times I felt quite rejected by her, as she seemed to distrust me when I interacted with them. I felt there was a sense of 'Well, he left my mother when she was pregnant, I don't trust him with my children.' I distinctly remember picking up Hollie for a piggyback and Jo watching me like a hawk and insisting I hold her a certain way. She didn't seem to believe I could do it my way, even though I'd raised three children of my own. The other thing I remember was her response to physical contact. I would always give her a hug whenever we met, but I initially got a stiff reaction from her, like she was uncomfortable with close body contact. She's become far more at ease with me over the years and I now understand that she wasn't held a lot as a child, but at the time I was conscious of it, although it was never an issue. So, in those small ways, I felt there were some barriers, but they were not major. It was a different relationship to what I had with my other children, but we reached the point a long time ago where it felt natural.

One thing I was always conscious of was that I didn't want to intrude on the relationship Jo had with her adoptive father. He'd been in her life longer than I had and I felt I needed to be sensitive to his feelings, nor, for example, would I contemplate moving closer to Jo while her adoptive father was still alive. I thought two fathers would be a burden to her and I didn't want him to feel at his stage of life that I was intruding.

I know it must have been tough for Jo's adoptive parents having us come back into her life when we did. I believe that adoptive parents have every right to feel possessive about their child because they don't have a choice about the birth family coming back on the scene. In my opinion it is only very open-minded adoptive parents who can let the child integrate back into the birth family.

Brigitta's partner Andrew

Being adopted wasn't really something Brigs talked about when we first met. I don't think it came up until she met my family and it was mentioned that my younger brother was adopted and she said something like, 'Oh, I'm adopted, too', and that's when she started talking to my brother about it. But generally, adoption wasn't a topic she spoke openly about. If the subject came up as to why she hadn't searched for her birthmother, she would say she had a family that loved her and raised her, and she had no need to look for anyone else. I think her denying she had any interest in her origins was a way of protecting herself, as well as the wish to protect her adoptive parents, particularly her father. She had a much stronger attachment to her father than to her adoptive mother, so she tended to subjugate her own feelings to protect him, although that changed as she got older and detached herself from her adoptive family.

When our eldest daughter was around six months old, Brigs raised the subject of her adoption, though still in an indirect way, by saying, 'I think it would be really good for Zoë to find out where she came from.' She tended to justify the search for her birthmother as something to do for the sake of the children, in case of any inherited health issues. She wasn't able to articulate any of her own needs yet, that took another two or three years, but when she finally said she wanted to search, I said I would support her. At that point her rationale became: 'If I'm going to do this, it's for my birthmother's sake, and for the girls', not mine.'

Brigs has loads of protection mechanisms and I could see the similarities in her talking about this subject and protecting herself from being hurt in other areas. If it didn't work out, she could say, 'I wasn't that interested in finding her anyway, it would have been nice for the kids, that's all.' The closer we got to the information we needed, the more honest Brigs became about the reasons she was doing it. There were more comments such as, 'Wouldn't it be great to find out some things about my birthmother,' and 'I wonder if I look like her.'

Ahead of the first meeting, I was very nervous for Brigs. Jan had sent some photos, but it is always different when you are face to face. I didn't want Brigs to get hurt. I knew it could potentially be very painful for her if there was a rejection of any kind. Brigs had expressed how she'd like it to go, and if it hadn't worked out that way, I think she'd have been very disappointed. I was quite anxious about this. Initially, Brigs said she wanted to do it on her own, but I wanted to be there, not only because I was curious but also in case things went pear-shaped.

This was such a novel position to be in because we were meeting someone for the first time, but there was already this important connection. It was very strange. We were lucky, though. Jan was amazing and I remember when she left saying to Brigs, 'She's cool', and it was true. I think if Jan hadn't been so open, Brigs would have continued to protect herself. It was only when she felt safe with Jan that she allowed herself to become more vulnerable, but it would take more than that first meeting to feel this way — she needed time.

Jan also protected herself. For months, even up until a year later, Jan kept saying, 'If at any point you don't want any more contact, if you feel like you've found out enough about me, then that would be fine.' I think this was her way of coping in case Brigs pulled back.

●

Thinking about the overall impact that being with an adopted person has had on our relationship, I feel the biggest issue is how Brigs handles conflict and rejection. The challenge is how her flight or fight instincts kick in when she is dealing with new situations, and the protection mechanisms she has developed as a result of being adopted. For example, if we get into a conflict, I'll want to get closer and explore what's going on, and Brigs's natural reaction is to want to pull back and protect herself. She has recognised that in herself now, so it's less of an issue, but during the early years I would get anxious because she'd start pulling back and this made me feel uncomfortable about our relationship. We now understand about patterns and behaviours in adopted people, and that protecting and withdrawing to avoid hurt is quite common. It's something that continues to come up, but it's easier to deal with because we know why it occurs.

I've had to learn not to take it personally when she pulls away and to realise that she's doing it because she is anxious to avoid further emotional hurt. I wasn't able to figure that out on my own; we needed to go to counselling together to work out what was going on. The biggest thing I got out of the therapy was the understanding that the way a person is behaving often has a lot more to do with what has happened to them in the past than what is occurring in the present. They're bringing maladaptive stuff into the relationship and applying it to the current situation. Just the simple process of recognising it is happening makes it easier to accept a behaviour.

Prior to this, my natural reaction was to think it was something I was doing. When it kept happening, my own protection mechanisms and anxiety kicked in, but now I think: 'She's doing that because of what's happened in the past and that is her issue. I've just got to be myself and support her through this, and hopefully she'll come back to me.'

I now know that for a lot of adopted people, their fear of rejection is manifested through neediness and a tendency to cling to their partner. Brigs is the opposite — she tends to isolate and remove herself. She withdraws rather than holding on tight. When everything is rosy and going well, she stays connected and quite balanced, but when things are challenging, she struggles to stay engaged and not walk away from things. And if anyone breaks her trust, that's it, they're out. She has this tendency to be very unforgiving of people if they hurt her or let her down, and I'm sure that stems from not wanting to be vulnerable with people.

She seems to find relationships with women quite tough. When I met her, she always had a lot more male friends, and she still seems to struggle with not getting hurt by other women. I know she worries about how strong her attachment is to our children, given that she had an interrupted attachment with her birthmother. I personally don't think this is an issue, though, as her awareness of this occurring in her past has allowed her to make conscious decisions about how she parents. She undertook huge amounts of research at every stage of the girls' development to try to make sure she got it right. But sometimes I think this worked against her, as she didn't tend to trust her natural instincts.

She could be hyper-vigilant around the emotional wellbeing of the girls. She's not uptight about their physical safety, but if one of them was having issues at school with friendships or something similar, she became quite personally affected by it, empathetic and emotional around their needs and deeply immersed. I would say that she genuinely feels their pain. Another thing I have noticed about how she parents, and the repercussions of being raised by her adoptive mother rather than her birthmother, is that she lacks confidence about how she should *be* as a mother. I had a strong attachment with my mother and a close relationship with her, so I intuitively knew what I wanted my children to feel from me as a parent. I had someone to learn from. I think Brigs has really had to try to figure it out by testing lots of different ways of parenting.

She used to beat herself up about how she was parenting. I think it was quite an entrenched fear of hers that she would get it wrong. From what I have learnt, it was more around her not being okay with who she was as a person, combined with a strong need to appear perfect at everything, striving and trying to take charge. I think this has at times stopped her from moving forward in some respects, and I know it is another reason she struggled with motherhood. Parenting is chaotic at times, but because she couldn't seem to relax about it, she found it hard to relinquish control and simply have fun with our children.

Brigs has talked about how she envies the level of contentment I have within myself. I feel like I'm mostly okay, whereas she is on a continual search for something to make herself happy and to prove her worth. She has an intense need for others to validate and approve of her, and for a long time growing up she felt she could only be loved through achievement.

Birthdays are an example of her need to be recognised and appreciated. She wants a big fuss made of her on her birthday and I wonder how much of that is to feed a sense of belonging.

Birthdays were not a big deal in my family, and I felt a sense of belonging anyway. If Brigs doesn't get treated as if she is special enough on her birthday, Mother's Day or our anniversary, she gets upset and takes it as a sign of rejection. It's almost as if she thinks I don't care or understand how important it is for her to be recognised on these occasions.

Alongside this is a desire to develop new traditions for us as a family. She's always dreaming up new rituals and ways to celebrate special occasions. I really enjoy most of these, but I don't have a need to create them myself. I think for Brigs there is a wish to establish a new identity for herself that is not governed by either her adoptive or her birth family, and new traditions are part of that.

Our daughters were quite young when Brigs first started writing about adoption, but I remember Jade summing it up nicely from her perspective when she said, 'Mummy, it's complicated being adopted, isn't it?'

Brigitta's daughter Zoë

I don't remember having a particular moment of awareness that our family was different to others due to Mum being adopted. To be honest, things had already felt slightly different with Granny and Grandpa David getting divorced, which was certainly an unusual dynamic compared to some of my friends' families.

We don't have much extended family on Mum's side, and because she's had a somewhat strained relationship with them, I never really enjoyed those gatherings. Mum's relationship with her adoptive mother was always tense, partly because of the kind of person Nana was and the issues this caused when Mum was growing up. When I was young, we didn't have a huge family Christmas like other kids did, but we had really good friendships with Mum and Dad's friends, so they were almost our substitute aunts and uncles. After we met Nanna Jan, and then Grandbob, I was so happy to feel part of a much larger family. I loved all the new cousins, aunties and uncles, plus I was proud to tell people that I had not four but eight people I considered to be my grandparents.

I think Mum has struggled a bit with feeling like she doesn't fit into either of her families, which can make her quite anxious in these situations, even when it is with Dad's family. Everyone else has grown up around each other and sort of knows their place. Even for me, I look like everyone else in Dad's family; I have shared heritage and I am one of the much-loved eldest grandchildren, but I am aware that Mum missed out on this on both sides of her family. I guess I did, too, to a certain extent, as I missed out on a history with Nanna Jan. I feel quite sad that she wasn't able to know me when I was little, as she is amazing with babies.

I had a very close relationship with Granny (Dad's mum), so having another grandmother come into my life as a child was certainly a change. I don't remember specifically meeting Nanna Jan, but that whole first weekend had positive connotations for me, and Nanna Jan made it extremely easy to trust her. I began to love her like my other grandparents right from the beginning. Moving to Hawke's Bay to be closer to her had a huge impact on my life. I remember going with Nanna Jan, the weekend before we moved, to visit my new school and to play on the school playground, and my class in Auckland writing me cards telling me to 'have a nice week in Napier', so I guess we were all confused about what was happening!

Although there were things that were difficult about this transition, I wouldn't have changed any of it. Living close to Nanna Jan and Poppa, as well as a new set of cousins with whom we became close through childhood, allowed us to strengthen a bond that couldn't have happened if we had stayed in Auckland. Holidays and weekends spent at the farm are some of my happiest childhood memories and I am so grateful we 'city slickers', as Poppa fondly called us, were able to experience rural life. Jade and I were treated as valued members of their extended family, we were asked questions, and there were adults interested in playing with us and having fun, which was really nice.

In terms of my maternal grandparents, Nanna Jan and Poppa were the more fun grandparents and have been perhaps more nurturing and warm than Nana and Grandpa were — who were already quite elderly when I was growing up. I've seen videos of me with Grandpa when I was little, and he was incredibly loving, I just can't remember, and I'm sorry that I never knew Grandpa in his prime. Then Poppa suffered from Alzheimer's in his later years, so I've missed having a loving male grandparent figure on Mum's side of the family, especially as I was always close to Poppa and had a huge amount of fun with him. I think it's made me even closer to Nanna Jan, since she's now living by herself; her home is my safe space in Hawke's Bay with Mum and Dad in Wellington, and all my friends know and call her Nanna Jan too.

Meeting Grandbob was very different because I was now older, so I fully understood the dynamics and the emotional baggage. I felt nervous but also protective of Nanna Jan and Mum, seeing as I knew the history behind Mum's conception. Bob had included us in his emails and we had messaged individually for about a year before visiting, meeting him in South Africa as part of our dream family holiday. I do remember on the flight over, I was sitting next to Mum and she was freaking out, so that was stressful. Then arriving in Cape Town, I had butterflies, I was so nervous, not knowing what Grandbob looked like or if he'd accept us, but for me, at least, it went perfectly and I loved getting to know him. I wish he lived closer so that I could properly establish a relationship with him, but unfortunately, we've gone back to just occasional emails in the years since that visit.

Nanna Jan coming on the scene certainly showed us a change in the way Mum interacted with a mother figure, but I have to say, as much as Mum and Nanna Jan try, I think it proves you can't get back lost years or have the same kind of secure relationship as you can with a parent you've grown up with since birth. Another thing that really stood out for me after their meeting up was how there was always some secret to remember or some information someone couldn't be told, such as who we were spending Christmas with, or not telling Nana Helen and Grandpa that we'd met Bob. I never liked this whole secretive dynamic, and it put a lot of strain on Mum. She often got very stressed during holiday times and on other significant occasions.

I definitely think dealing with emotions about both her

adoptive and birth families has been really difficult for Mum. Now that I'm an adult, it's hard to juggle these relationships when I've wanted to keep the peace between Mum and various family members because she has a tendency to withdraw from people when everything isn't going perfectly. When I was younger, there was always this sense that something could easily go wrong and Jade and I both responded to the tense atmosphere. A few years ago we had a big family Christmas at our place, and everyone was coming. I remember being nervous about how it was going to go, and Mum and I had an argument that night, which I now understand was Mum letting off some steam. I didn't recognise it in the moment as I'm quite reactive myself, but later I realised she'd been on edge all day, and it wasn't an attack on me personally.

It was worse when it was Mum and her adoptive mother, but Mum wasn't that securely attached to either of her mothers; it looked more like how she'd interact with any adult, not like a mother–daughter relationship at all. It was definitely different to my relationship with my mother who gave birth to me and who I grew up with, even though we've had our issues.

I think Mum was very unsure of herself as a parent and she worried a lot about that. Parenting didn't seem to come naturally to her, and she jumped between parenting styles — she was hard to read rather than being steady and stable. I think it made it difficult for me to be sure of myself when my mother, someone I am so strongly influenced by, was not being steady — it was hard to figure out how I needed to be on certain days. I would have loved for her to really get to grips with parenting and accept that kids are messy and complicated, to just hug and play with us, and be as warm and loving as possible, without trying to be perfect.

I think Mum tried very hard to make us feel loved and to hold space for us to be as close to her as possible — almost to the extreme — whereas Dad's parenting style came a lot more easily to him. Mum didn't have that natural maternal instinct because she wasn't shown it from her own mother. She worked hard at being maternal and being a good mum, but she never seemed to trust her instincts. I definitely have a different relationship with her to the one I have with Dad; he's always been a lot more solid, a real rock, as opposed to Mum who was up and down all the time — but Mum had to try to figure this role out all on her own.

Mum was a different kind of mum to my friends' mothers. She wasn't the kind to do home baking or commit her entire life to her kids, which I actually admire her for, as all through our upbringing she had her own personal goals and expectations, which set her in good stead for Jade and me leaving home. Dad, on the other hand, although also career-focused, has struggled a lot more since we left home because I think he was a lot more attached to us than Mum was.

Mum and I are both strong-willed, we know what we want and so we tend to butt heads because of this. I'm not sure if it is just part of her personality, or whether it's because she had to forge her own way in the world to a certain extent, but she can kind of retreat or pull away when something doesn't go right or someone disagrees with her. Mum doesn't trust very easily, and she is quick to lose trust in others. You do not want to get on her bad side, because she will hate you for the rest of your life! Even if one of my friends has done something to me — including times way back in my childhood — Mum will never forgive them, because she won't trust them anymore.

Brigitta's daughter Jade

I feel like Mum being adopted has made her doubt herself quite a lot. She doubts her parenting and how she is as a mother. She doesn't always feel like she's good enough. Sometimes she'll make comments about her parenting where it feels like she wants reassurance, and I know a lot of adopted people don't feel wanted. But she's been an amazing mother despite that. I honestly don't feel that I've been affected by her being adopted really, not in a way I can see, anyway. She's mostly been just a normal parent — a really cool one. Mum has been so supportive of everything we do and encouraged us to try new things, to do our own thing, and she always made a big effort to be there for every sports game and commitment we had. I feel like she was as protective as any 'normal' parent and wasn't overly protective, which was good.

Even though I was really little, I remember when we first met Nanna Jan, then we visited her at her farm, and I don't recall being nervous or anything because she was just so welcoming and always really nice to me. Mum never really made a big deal about our family being a bit different and she didn't talk about it much. When Nanna Jan came along, Nana and Grandpa were still my 'full' grandparents no matter what, so that didn't feel any different either.

I liked having lots of grandparents. Grandpa was really nice and Nana looked after me — it was lovely having them close by when they moved down from Auckland, but I did a lot more with Poppa and Nanna Jan; I'd look forward to doing fun activities with them as they were younger. Nanna Jan spoiled us a lot. I always felt really comfortable at her place — I remember falling asleep on her couch when I was little. When Grandbob came into our lives, I remember being on the plane going to meet him and asking Mum if she was nervous. I don't think I was nervous. Grandbob was funny and I liked his whole family. I had a really good time in South Africa.

Nanna Jan and Nana would talk quite a lot and hang out together at family occasions. Grandpa was getting quite old then, so I don't recall him being involved in the conversations, but Poppa was always quite chatty. It was kind of weird. I would find myself thinking about the past at these times and not be able to get my head around the fact that they knew of each other but had never met. It never felt normal seeing the two grandmothers together. They had that history, but to see them chatting, all those years later, was something that didn't make sense to me. It still doesn't.

I remember Mum telling us how there was a 10-day period when her birthmother had to make a decision and then at the end of that time Mum got picked up and her two brothers were there in the car. Nanna Jan told me she remembered looking down at the car — I don't know if they ever met then — but when I hear that story it makes me feel really sad. I find it upsetting and emotional. She must have felt so lonely, and then she used to go to the primary schools to see if she could see Mum. It makes me cry. I think Nanna Jan is so happy that we are in her life, although I don't know what she really feels about what happened back then. Mum had a good life and was successful, and I think she is happy Mum had siblings, but I'm not sure how she felt about Nana being bipolar or what effect that had on Mum; she must wonder if she could have raised her differently or whether it would have been better if she hadn't given her away.

I think it was hard for Mum growing up with Nana. It would be hard for me if my mum wasn't very present. Maybe that's why our mum has always been so supportive of us — she perhaps wanted to be different. But I also think Mum hasn't been that affectionate with us because she wasn't shown this from her own mother. Mum made a conscious effort to be supportive, she just wasn't all that affectionate with hugs and kisses, but she did other things differently to how she was raised. I'm fine with it the way it is; I'm not super affectionate myself and don't like being too 'huggy' with my friends, for example. Some of my friends' families are really affectionate with each other, saying 'I love you' non-stop, even when they leave a room. If I'm feeling sad, Mum is more understanding now than she was when we were younger. In the past if we were in an argument it would always be her way, and she would never apologise because she thought she was right all the time, which wasn't great.

I think Mum's relationship with each of her two mothers has been quite different. With Nanna Jan, she was quite bossy. I always noticed it and I don't know why she was, but she was quite controlling. Maybe because Nanna Jan is always so nice and will do what she's told and Mum didn't know how to deal with this because her adoptive mother was such a different personality. Sometimes Nanna Jan can be too nice, too careful, and I know Mum can get a bit frustrated by this. But with Nana, the two of them were more on the same level; she'd grown up with her being her mother and Mum never acted in that dominant way, although I remember her getting upset with her, mainly around Nana being inconsiderate. She could be quite rude to Mum and I didn't like that. But Mum's never been all that affectionate with either of her mothers; she'd give them a hug when she saw them but that was about it.

When I have my own kids, I want to make sure I'm really close with them and that they can tell me anything. I would never want to adopt a child myself. One of my friends is adopted, and I know it depends on the situation, but I've seen how it can have an impact on you. I just want to have a family where everyone is biologically related — the simplicity of that is appealing, compared to how complex it has been for Mum.

Jo's partner Lawrie

Since I have known Jo, our relationship has been influenced and shaped by the fact that she was adopted. It was a large part of who she was when we met as teenagers. I met Jo's adoptive parents when I was 15 years old, then they became my in-laws, whom I loved and respected, and we have always been very close as a family, sharing many times together over the years. They were fantastic grandparents to our two children, helping us raise them, especially in the early years when Jo and I both worked to pay the mortgage. When my mother-in-law died, Jo's dad and I shared a meal together once or twice a week. To me, they are and always will be Jo's parents.

However, it was very clear to me and our friends, even at the ripe old age of 15, that Jo looked different, behaved differently, and she wanted different things to her parents. Jo was a bit of a rebel at school, pushing the boundaries in terms of her behaviour, and she was not afraid to buck the system. On the other hand, I was often teased for being a 'goody good', yet here I became attracted to this young woman who had heaps of energy and didn't comply as I did. She was a ball of fun and beautiful and I wanted to be in on the action. So, one month before her sixteenth birthday, I borrowed a friend's motorbike, took her for a ride and asked her to be my girlfriend.

Jo did little study and did not apply herself much at school. She didn't seem interested in learning and when it came to her classes her concentration span was short. She wanted answers, not to questions about mathematical formula or historical events or how butterflies grow inside cocoons but to questions such as: Who am I? Where did I come from? Why am I different to the rest of my family? When Jo was trying to figure these life issues out, she was discouraged, with the implication being: 'It is what it is and be grateful for that.'

At 17, Jo wanted to search for her birthmother, but I had an overwhelming feeling that this was a massive step to take and we were too young to go on such a journey. I didn't know much about adoption back then, but when Jo went through difficult emotional periods, it brought about in her a longing to know. In those early years of our relationship, I did not understand or appreciate what she was feeling or going through, and certainly I had no idea of the pain she felt, yet I promised Jo that when she turned 21, I would help her search. Subconsciously, I probably felt that by then Jo would be over this madness, over her emotional teenage years, over the issues that plagued her, and all would be rosy. Little did I know back then that Jo never forgets a promise and, of course, the legacy of adoption is always there.

In those early years, it was clear that Jo was looking for something. She wanted to be with me or our friends all the time; she wanted constant contact and connection. If I didn't make myself available to her, she would feel rejected and would question my level of love for her. At times I felt I was walking on eggshells. If I said or did the wrong thing, like not phoning her when she was expecting me to, she would be hurt. I clearly enjoyed being with Jo, but I was also busy playing sport, studying, hanging out with my mates and being a typical teenager. Jo was needy in a way that our other female friends were not, and at times this was stressful. I had to compromise on things that I wanted to do in order to keep her happy, or I would simply do what I wanted to do and if this didn't involve her, she would become upset with me. It would take us many years to understand fully the legacy of adoption and the implications on our relationship.

Just before Jo turned 21, she posted the letter to Jigsaw and the search was now on. I was very concerned and worried that we might walk into an ugly situation. Her birthmother could have died, or perhaps she wouldn't want to know, or she could be living in unpleasant circumstances, and therefore Jo would get hurt once again. Which was better: knowing or not knowing? Jo had a hunger to find the answers to her questions, but I kept thinking about the implications if what she found wasn't good. Then that *Dominion Post* advertisement was printed and it was a shock and a wake-up call that this dream of Jo's might in fact come true. So many years of longing and now we knew someone had been thinking about Jo for probably all the 21 years of her life. There was possibly a member of her birth family searching for her, and maybe Jo would get the answers she needed. She wouldn't get hurt because both sides wanted contact. If they were good people, they wouldn't reject this beautiful, fun-loving woman.

Jo was to meet her birth grandmother on her own. I was so nervous, but trying not to show this to Jo, while she was just a wreck! I thought her heart was about to explode. I could hear it pounding from the other end of our house. The meeting with Jo's grandmother went extremely well and I could not stop thinking how lucky we were. Jo was given lots of information. It was particularly wonderful to discover that Jo's birthparents had been in love with each other but were just too young to raise her. Also knowing that they were still alive was hugely comforting. For the first time Jo heard that being put up for adoption was not her fault. Theory is one thing, but to know the actual circumstances of your own adoption changes your perception of yourself. Knowing the truth about this was such an important part of Jo's healing.

Then it was time to meet Jo's birthfather, Tony. I was not as nervous this time as we now had a lot of information about him. At this stage we were aware that neither Tony nor Sue had been looking for Jo, so I was worried how he felt about meeting her when it was not something he had instigated or probably had ever considered. So, this time I went with Jo. I thought it would be quite a formal meeting, a shake of the hand, some discussions on what we had done in our lives, a cup of tea, a goodbye and then off.

We saw Tony as we drove up the driveway to his home. He looked tall, strong, handsome and was smiling. I remember he held Jo's hand for long periods of time. It seemed a bit weird, as we didn't know him, but almost instantly there was a connection between the two of them. It was not like meeting a stranger for the first time. It was a unique meeting between a father and his daughter. There was an unspoken bond uniting them, a birthparent to their child. The way Tony embraced Jo and his calming influence helped both Jo and me relax and take in this whole experience. We were in this surreal situation, there were plenty of nerves, a realisation that we were in the presence of Tony, her birthfather, and there was no rejection. Then came the bombshell: Sue was flying over from Australia. I was knocked off my feet. I remember saying to Jo, 'This is happening too fast.' But it was taken out of our control and we simply could not say no.

My memory of the first meeting with Sue is hazy. Tony was chatty, but I don't recall that Sue spoke much. My first impression was how similar Sue and Jo were in height, body shape and similar-looking faces. It was obvious to me that Sue was Jo's birthmother. In the evening, the plan was to have dinner together. For much of Jo's life she had fantasised about this. Both birthparents in her life! She was now beginning to learn where she came from, why she looked like she did, and her birth family's history — things like health issues that might affect Jo in the future, information about her half brothers and sister and why she was good at sport when her adoptive parents were not.

But when we received a call to say Sue would not be joining us for dinner, that she couldn't cope, I just couldn't believe it. I couldn't understand how someone could travel all this way from Australia then not follow through. Naturally, we had no idea what Sue herself was going through, but Jo was devastated. It was like she'd had this little taste and then it was gone. Jo's birth grandmother tried to explain to us why Sue reacted the way she did, but it was of little consolation to Jo. She cried for hours. Then she became angry. Her feelings of rejection swelled. I think she wanted to have a connection with Sue that she didn't have with her mum. She wanted the mother–daughter connection that she saw between her younger sister and her adoptive mother.

After that first meeting, Sue was very reserved and not a 'motherly' type. Jo didn't think she could express her needs to Sue, as she didn't want Sue to feel uncomfortable, so talking about her feelings was not an option. The relationship was kept on a friendship level, not because Jo wanted it that way, but because she felt Sue might not cope with anything else.

●

Having been married to Jo for 40 years, I think the biggest challenge in our relationship has been the way we have dealt with her feelings of abandonment and rejection. That second rejection from Sue triggered all sorts of stuff that had been impacting on Jo since she was born, and on us both in our own relationship. I never understood the feelings Jo had. I saw how she reacted, but I never connected with them and often I simply didn't want to know. I just wanted Jo to sort herself out. It took many years for me to appreciate that such feelings of rejection and abandonment are not like having a common cold. You can't take some Panadol and they'll go away.

Through my teens, twenties and into my thirties, I would do the things I wanted and I acted in a way I felt was normal. Often, I didn't know what I had done to upset Jo, other than perhaps not return a phone call, or not be present when she wanted to talk, or go out playing cricket or rugby while leaving her to care for the children. Jo wanted relationship and connection regularly in her daily life, but I was not often there for her as I've never had a need to be called up just to see how my day is going. Connection in relationships is of major importance to Jo. Perhaps as a male and having been raised by my birthparents — so, knowing who I was and where I came from — I have not needed others on this same level. For Jo and I, our levels of need were at different ends of the scale.

Because so many of Jo's needs had not been met by her adoptive family, she brought this neediness to our relationship. She constantly searched for relationships with friends and family that would fulfil the needs unmet when she was a child. For many years her dependence on me made me feel adored on the one hand but challenged on the other. There were times when I wanted to escape, to get out of the house, to not feel weighed down by Jo's neediness. There were occasions when I let her down by not being more aware or by not wanting to become aware of what life was like for an adopted person.

In the past, when I saw Jo struggling, I would try to fix the problem. By fixing it, surely the problem would go away. This of course was not the answer. Instead of just listening and being empathetic, I would give to her what I thought was a solution, or otherwise minimise the issue. It took many years for me to realise that such a response was never going to make her happy. What she needs from me is to truly listen to her express her feelings of rejection, abandonment or hurt, to validate her feelings and to support her in reaching her own way of resolving things.

Over the years Jo has learnt through her own personal development how to meet her needs and she has passed this knowledge on to me. I no longer feel the weight of the burden that I once felt. Jo is a vastly different person today from who she was. The personal development she has undertaken has given her a strong sense of self. She fully trusts her own judgement on matters and issues that arise in her life, while her strong sense of self means that if she gets a gut feeling about something, she is invariably right.

At times Jo can still struggle in friendships, particularly with women. Jo always gives 100 per cent to her close relationships and many people struggle to reciprocate at the same level, so there is an imbalance, and at times she will feel hurt because she gives so much more. She may withdraw for a while and those who are affected don't understand what is wrong. However, these days, this is rarely an issue.

For many years Jo's birthday was significant and it was always a very emotional day. Whoever contacted her would be in favour and whoever didn't were not. Both our children have been exceptionally good at making contact or getting cards to her on her birthday, but if they or other people close to Jo didn't make contact, then it would upset her. Jo used to go overboard on other people's birthdays, determined to make people feel important and loved on their special day.

Jo quickly bounces back now that she has a better understanding of the issues that have affected her over the years. Although she still has these feelings every now and then, she is equipped with the tools to work out whether her feelings are due to patterns in the past or whether there is a real issue to be resolved.

Jo tends to still need projects to work on — when one is finished, she looks for the next. With her having spent many years on her personal development, however, she has become less burdened and has discovered a thirst for learning. This led to her spending two years studying for her master's degree at Oxford Brookes University in the United Kingdom.

Her personal journey has given her inner peace and has enabled her to feel safe and have confidence in her own beliefs. Jo is leading a flourishing life. Perhaps, more importantly, she is now self-reliant, while at the same time, we have the emotional connection between us that a husband and wife should have. Jo can now live on her own for long periods of time, as she did when completing her studies in London, and for four years when she lived and worked mostly in Wellington while I was based in Napier.

One of the most important strategies for being in a relationship with an adopted person is having knowledge of the issues that affect adopted people. Once you accept and understand the reasons behind the behaviour, or the feelings they express, you can then learn ways to deal with it. My responding to Jo appropriately is what enhances our relationship. It was Jo's total commitment to our relationship that got us through earlier years when I didn't understand and didn't have the skills to support her. In similar circumstances, many relationships would have ended.

Jo's children Will and Hollie

From a young age we both knew that Mum was adopted, but it didn't really mean that much until we got older. The main impression we had was how different she felt she was from her adoptive family. Her birthparents seemed to have a lot of similar personality traits to her while her adoptive parents did not.

She didn't seem to particularly struggle with being adopted when we were growing up, but it was always clear that she was very different from the family that raised her. They were a more serious kind of family than we were, and Mum would sometimes make comments about that. Mum's adoptive family didn't seem to have a lot of fun together — it was all about service to others and the church — whereas Mum has always got a lot of enjoyment out of life.

The story of how Mum came to meet her birthparents Tony and Sue was quite a nice one, so there was a positive connotation around searching for and finding her birth family. Initially, Tony and Sue weren't around much when we were young, but they did become more involved as we got older. There were never any negative feelings about adoption because it was always openly discussed in our family.

Tony and Sue were quite independent types, whereas Mum has always been very family oriented, and those bonds are important to her. But in lots of other ways she was like them. She used to get excited when she realised there was an element of Sue's behaviour or a family trait that she recognised in herself. That was quite a big deal to her. In terms of our relationship with them, they weren't really on an equal par with Grandma and Grandad. Tony and Sue were living remotely, so we only saw them for a couple of days here and there. They weren't a major influence in our lives growing up as they didn't take the same interest or have the level of involvement Mum's adoptive parents did. They were more like good family friends than grandparents.

There was a stage, however, when Sue, in particular, seemed to become much more involved in Mum's life. Maybe that was around the time that Grandma died, and she finally felt she wasn't overstepping boundaries, and Mum became much happier as Sue became involved. She would go and stay with her and things like that.

Mum really sheltered us from the major stuff she was going through with her adoption journey. Dad wore most of it and was 100 per cent behind her. She never showed us how upset she was. She tried to make sure we liked both her birthparents and her adoptive parents. I don't remember Mum being negative about anyone. She would point out the differences and she would make comments, but never in any way that would make us feel negatively about anyone in the family.

The biggest difference we saw in Mum to other parents was the fear she had around something happening to us.

This impacted on what she allowed us to do because her first instinct was always to be overly protective. There was a big contrast between what parents of friends and Dad would let us do compared to what Mum was comfortable with. She had this irrational fear of losing us, and perhaps it stemmed back to the separation with her mother when she was a baby, but she always went one step further to try to protect us. We both know there is a reason for it now, but as kids we felt we were too protected growing up. If we were climbing trees or walking on ledges, she would tell us to get down or hold her hand. She was always worried about us hurting ourselves, always worried that we were going to do something stupid. She was really anxious.

Getting emotional about things was a big part of Mum's personality. She's very sensitive and there were times when we felt she was overreacting to certain things. She always cried at movies, but also when we were teenagers and behaving badly; instead of just telling us off, she would often cry. Sometimes it would make us feel guilty. Other times we would wonder what on earth we'd done to set her off. It could be quite bewildering to try to figure out why she was having such an emotional reaction. It didn't always happen, and that was part of the problem, because with Dad you always knew where you stood, but with Mum you never quite knew if something would trigger her or not.

She is less emotional now, but she can still worry. She used to need us to immediately reply if she was trying to contact us. When we've been travelling and living overseas and we've been out of contact for a while, before we know it, we get bombarded with calls, emails and text messages asking what has happened and checking if we are still alive. If you didn't respond within a day, she'd go into overdrive, and we've both had to say at times, 'Mum, you're taking it too far.' Compared with other parents, she was over the top in her need to be in constant contact and her fears of what might happen to us.

Dad's always been a huge support to her, and he's had to wear a lot of the same stuff that we've found hard to deal with at times — the fears and the overprotectiveness. She relied on Dad to be there and to reassure her, and he's done a really good job of being that support so it didn't place too much of a burden on us. He was her rock, but she did need reassurance from us too when he wasn't around. She used to get anxious when she didn't have access to us, and that ties back to her need to stay in regular contact. With Dad you could go a month without talking to him and he would be fine, but Mum needs more contact.

However, she has always been a very loving and caring mother. We have felt close to both our parents. Mum was certainly always there for us and we could talk to her about anything. She would always give good advice and there was never any doubt how much she loved us.

Above: Brigitta aged six with her brothers and Snowy the cat (devouring a wild rabbit); Brigitta dancing at her wedding with her adopted dad in Christchurch, 2000.

Below: Brigitta's daughters Jade and Zoë with their grandpa on his eightieth birthday.

Above: Jade, Zoë and Nanna Jan celebrating Jade's fifth birthday in Auckland, 2009.
Below: Brigitta with her birthfather Bob in Hawke's Bay when he visited New Zealand in 2017.

Above: Jo's adoptive family in Piopio, 1963 (from left): Jo's brother Alex, adoptive mother Noeline, Jo, and her adoptive father Keith; Peggy, Jo's paternal birth grandmother.

Below: Jo, her adoptive father Keith, sister Rhonda, adoptive mother Noeline and brother Alex at Jo's adoptive grandparents' fiftieth wedding anniversary celebrations in Napier in 1973.

Above: Jo's husband Lawrie, birthmother Sue, birthfather Tony and Jo, in Auckland.

Below: Five generations of the family in Tauranga in 2016: Jo's son Will, Jo, Jo's maternal grandmother Shirley holding Will's son Jack for the first time, several months before she passed away, and Jo's birthmother Sue.

Afterword

We have shared two very different versions of the New Zealand adoption experience. As babies, we were separated from our mothers and handed to strangers, and eventually, through the tumultuous journey of searching and reunion, we found our way back to our families of origin. But there are more commonalities than there are contrasts. It has been well recognised that to have access to knowledge about your lineage and your place in the world is vital to your wellbeing and sense of self. But those of us born during the closed adoption era were denied this most basic human right, and the repercussions of that denial have reverberated throughout our lives.

Everything we have related in this book is our perspective at the time the events took place, and illustrates the issues and events that were real for us. It reflects what we felt in the moment, but it doesn't necessarily mean that we were right, or that those feelings still stand today.

We have chosen to focus on us, on the legacy of closed adoption and the journey of reunion we took, and to a lesser extent our birthparents. Both our adoptive fathers passed away during the writing of this book, and although they and one of our adoptive mothers were interviewed as part of our research, we have not focused specifically on the personal stories of our adoptive parents. This does not in any way dismiss the critical role of adoptive families, nor does it minimise the degree of challenge they also face through the reunion process.

Even when reunion is achieved, our stories illustrate how relationships are often highly complex and difficult to navigate. There are no maps to negotiate them. There may be a genetic likeness, but initially the parties are unknown to each other, and it can be extremely difficult to figure out what each person wants from the other, unless there is an opportunity to talk about expectations openly and honestly.

Relationships in the post-reunion phase commonly seem to fall down or fail to meet the expectations of the parties involved. Many adopted people experience heightened sensitivity to rejection, which can make them more likely to pull back from their birth family when they feel they're being left out of decisions or their feelings are being overlooked; simple miscommunication can become more significant than warranted.

For birthparents, it can sometimes be too painful to 'let in' the relationship. They have often kept the door to their experience closed for so long, and buried their feelings so deep, that it can be extremely traumatic to confront the past and open themselves up to further emotional upheaval.

Reunion is often characterised by two wounded parties coming together, both of whom have been emotionally trapped at a developmental stage due to the trauma each has experienced through their early separation. The birthmother meets her child as an adult, and it can bring back memories of the birthfather, a broken relationship and the pain of relinquishment. The adopted person might have denied they were looking for an emotional attachment, but there is still a small baby inside who lost a mother and needs her on some level.

If the feelings of loss and grief associated with separation are unresolved when they meet, it can be extremely difficult to forge a relationship. It takes real courage and tenacity to work through the strong emotions triggered by reunion. Adopted people who have initiated the search may have to deal with the fact that their birthparents would never have looked for them. There can be a hurt associated with this that often needs to be overcome and forgiven in order to move forward openly with the relationship. For those adopted people who did not search, feelings of resentment that their previously stable existence has been overturned are natural. Their birthparent may appear too needy and they may want to distance themselves from someone they see as a stranger.

An awareness of the range of emotions being felt and a willingness to keep communicating and making decisions together can lead to positive, long-term outcomes for all parties involved — even when initially there may be a strong temptation to pull back.

Our stories are two of so many, but in telling them, our hope is to illuminate the journey that can be taken and to discover that adoption is not the only story. As we 'wake up' to and release the blocks from this experience, we begin to find wholeness in our broken places. We return home to our authentic self and, in time, find ourselves thriving, not simply surviving.

Appendices

Appendix A: A brief overview of adoption in New Zealand

New Zealand has a long history of adoption and, as a nation, it could be described as a country of prolific adopters. Adoption legislation was originally passed in 1881, making New Zealand the first country in the British Empire to regulate legal adoption.[1] Following the Second World War, the practice of 'closed stranger adoption', where young babies were adopted by parents unknown to the birth family, was strongly promoted by government agencies, and became the dominant form of adoption. Traditional Māori adoption, usually known as whāngai, where a child remained within the whānau but was not predominantly raised by the birthparents, continued as a common custom.

Before the war, total adoptions remained well below 1000 per year; however, in 1944 they began to exceed 1000. In 1955, when there were 1455 adoptions, 984 of them were by strangers.[2]

---

1 Bronwyn Dalley, *Family Matters: Child Welfare in Twentieth-century New Zealand*, Auckland: Auckland University Press, 1998.
2 The first year for which statistics for adoptions by strangers are available is 1955.

The numbers of stranger adoptions rose rapidly each year until 1972, when they reached a peak of 2286. They then started declining, and were down to 845 by 1979.[3] If you take into account not only the number of adopted children this involved but also their birth and adoptive parents, siblings, grandparents and other extended family, the overall impact of adoption on society and family structures was enormous.

The period from 1950 to the mid-1970s was a boom time for closed adoptions in New Zealand. All parties involved genuinely believed that what they were doing was in the best interests of the child, and the ideal environment in which to raise any child was described by the authorities of the time as a 'permanent home with breadwinning father and a stay-at-home mother'.[4] Closed adoption was a means of ensuring this societal ideal was achieved.

One of the key pieces of legislation created during this period, which still governs adoption practice today, is the Adoption Act 1955. The Act was introduced partly to protect adopted children from the stigma of illegitimacy. To achieve this, it effectively sealed all official records relating to the identities of the parties involved, making it virtually impossible for adopted children and their birthparents to have any future contact. This formalised the growing 'cult of secrecy' that surrounded the subject of adoption, and led to some of its most damaging repercussions.

---

3   See Anne Else, *A Question of Adoption: Closed Stranger Adoption in New Zealand*, 1944–1974, Wellington: Bridget Williams Books, 1991, Table 1, p. xii.
4   Dalley, *Family Matters*.

The passing of the Adult Adoption Information Act 1985 allowed adopted people over the age of 20 to gain access to their original birth certificate, and provided birthparents with a process through which they could contact their relinquished children. Nevertheless, it failed to counter the legacy of secrecy and denial that characterised closed adoption.

Key legislative changes affecting adoption in New Zealand since 1985 were the Children, Young Persons, and Their Families Act 1989 (now the Oranga Tamariki Act), which initiated the family-group conferencing model of decision-making for children in need of care or protection. Although the Act gave statutory weight to decision-making for children led by the family, whānau, hapū or iwi, it remains at odds with a parent or guardian's entitlement to confidentially place their child for adoption under the 1955 Act.

Intercountry adoption, which developed from 1990, was drawn into a more regulated framework when the 1997 Adoption (Intercountry) Act was created, consistent with the Hague Convention on Protection of Children and Co-operation in Respect of Intercountry Adoption, which aims to protect children and their families from trafficking and illegal and ill-prepared adoptions.

From the mid-1980s, social-work practice in New Zealand developed on the basis of an acceptance that closed stranger adoption did not work to the benefit of adopted people or their birthmothers. While the law did not change, open adoption from that time was promoted, and became the norm for those few children whose parents placed them for adoption by strangers each year. For the last decade or so, Oranga Tamariki has been involved in facilitating between 20 and 30 non-kin adoptions each year, while during the past 40 years, assisted reproductive technology has continued to offer couples and individuals increased options for forming a family outside of adoption.

In 2016, the Human Rights Commission found that New Zealand's adoption laws were 'discriminatory and outdated',[5] and consistently there have been calls for law reform to better reflect the interests of the people affected by adoption. Despite several attempts to initiate law reform — most notably the Law Commission's 2000 report, *Adoption and its Alternatives* — none of these efforts had yet come to fruition by 2020. However, in June 2021 the Ministry of Justice finally put out a discussion paper on comprehensive reform of adoption law.[6]

Appendix B: Adoption resources

There is a wealth of information available on adoption and reunion, and it is constantly being added to and updated. Further reading can be found in the bibliography, and includes several titles that can help answer questions that might have come up for you while reading *Adopted*. The following website may also be a useful starting point, particularly within the New Zealand context.

---

5 www.hrc.co.nz/news/human-rights-commission-calls-urgent-reform-new-zealand-adoption-laws.
6 www.justice.govt.nz/assets/Documents/Publications/Adoption-in-Aotearoa-NZ-Discussion-doc.pdf.

Adoption services — Oranga Tamariki: Adoptions in New Zealand, including services to assist finding information about both birthparents and adopted people, are coordinated by Oranga Tamariki, the Ministry for Children (formerly known as the Department of Child, Youth and Family Services). For more information, call 0508 326 459, or email webadoption@ot.govt.nz. Visit www.orangatamariki.govt.nz/adoption.

Further reading

Arnott, Paul. *A Good Likeness: A Personal Story of Adoption.* London: Little, Brown and Company, 2000.

Bowlby, John. *Attachment and Loss* (Vol. III: Loss). New York: Basic Books, 1980.

Brown, Brené. *I Thought It Was Just Me: Telling the Truth About Perfectionism, Inadequacy and Power.* New York: Gotham Books, 2007.

Brown, Brené. *The Gifts of Imperfection: Let Go of Who You Think You're Supposed to Be and Embrace Who You Are.* Center City: Hazelden Publishing, 2010.

Campbell, Joseph. *The Hero's Journey: Joseph Campbell on His Life and Work.* New York: HarperCollins Publishers, 1990.

Campbell, Nicky. *Blue-eyed Son: The Story of an Adoption.* London: Macmillan, 2004.

Carroll, Lewis. *Alice's Adventures in Wonderland.* New York: Macmillan, 1865.

Chopra, Deepak, Debbie Ford and Marianne Williamson. *The Shadow Effect: Illuminating the Hidden Power of Your True Self.* New York: HarperOne, 2010.

Coles, Gary. *Ever After: Fathers and the Impact of Adoption.* Christies Beach: Clova Publications, 2004.

Cooper, Robyn. *Don't Ask Her Name: An Adoption Story.* Whatamango Bay: Cape Catley, 1988.

Dalley, Bronwyn. *Family Matters: Child Welfare in Twentieth-Century New Zealand.* Auckland: Auckland University Press, 1998.

Darling, Stew. *Lead Through Life: A Fresh Approach to Leadership.* Australia: Ocean Reeve Publishing, 2020.

Dunn, Jean (ed). *Healing in the Truth: A Collection of Adoption Stories.* Whanganui: Whanganui Adoption Support Group NZ, 2006.

Eastman, P. D. *Are You My Mother?* New York: Random House, 1960.

Else, Anne. *A Question of Adoption: Closed Stranger Adoption in New Zealand 1944–1974.* Wellington: Bridget Williams Books, 1991. In 2022 a new digital edition of this history will be available from Bridget Williams Books, updated to cover the 30 years from 1991 to 2021. As well as adoption, it deals with the history of assisted reproductive technology involving donated eggs, sperm, embryos and surrogacy.

Gillard-Glass, Sheryn, and Jan England. *Adoption New Zealand: The Never-ending Story.* Auckland: HarperCollins Publishers, 2002.

Grant, Ian, and Mary Grant. *Growing Great Girls.* Auckland: Random House, 2008.

Griffith, Keith C. *The Right to Know Who You Are: Reform of Adoption Law with Honesty, Openness and Integrity.* Ottawa: Katherine W. Kimbell, 1991.

Hanson, Rick, and Richard Mendius. *Buddha's Brain: The Practical Neuroscience of Happiness, Love and Wisdom.* Oakland: New Harbinger Publications, 2009.

Harris, Russ. *The Happiness Trap: How to Stop Struggling and Start Living.* Boston: Trumpeter Books, 2007.

Henderson, Carol, and Heather Tovey. *Searching for Grace: A Woman's Quest for Her True Identity.* Wellington: Steele Roberts, 2010.

Hendrix, Harville, and Helen LaKelly Hunt. *Getting the Love You Want: A Guide for Couples, 20th Anniversary Edition.* New York: Holt Paperbacks, 2008.

Holm, Rod. *Rewriting the Script: An Adoption Story.* Palmerston North: Dunmore Press, 1994.

Homes, A. M. *The Mistress's Daughter.* New York: Penguin, 2008.

Horney, Karen. *Neurosis and Human Growth: The Struggle Towards Self-realisation.* London: Routledge & Kegan Paul, 1951.

Howarth, Ann. *Reunion: Adoption and the Search for Birth Origins — The New Zealand Story.* Auckland: Penguin Books, 1988.

Jarrell Bailey, Julie, and Lynn Giddens. *The Adoption Reunion Survival Guide: Preparing Yourself for The Search, Reunion, and Beyond.* Oakland: New Harbinger Publications, 2001.

Joseph, Stephen, and P. Alex Linley. *Positive Therapy: A Meta-theory for Positive Psychological Change.* Hove: Routledge, 2006.

Jung, C. G. *Modern Man in Search of a Soul.* New York: Harcourt, Brace & World, 1933.

Kehoe, John. *Mind Power: Techniques to Harness the Astounding Powers of Thought.* Canada: Transcontinental Printing, 1997.

Martin, Beryl. *A Family from Barra: An Adoption Story.* Auckland: Auckland University Press, 1997.

Muller, Wayne. *How Then, Shall We Live?: Four Simple Questions that Reveal the Beauty and Meaning of Our Lives.* New York: Bantam Books, 1997.

Pool, Ian, Arunachalam Dharmalingam, and Janet Sceats. *The New Zealand Family from 1840: A Demographic History.* Auckland: Auckland University Press, 2007.

Rainer, Tristine. *The New Diary.* New York: Tarcher, 1978.

Robinson, Evelyn B. *Adoption and Loss: The Hidden Grief.* South Australia: Clova Publications, 2000.

Rogers, C. *On Becoming a Person: A Therapist's View of Psychotherapy.* Boston: Houghton Mifflin, 1961.

Shawyer, Joss. *Death by Adoption.* Auckland: Cicada Press, 1979.

Verrier, Nancy Newton. *Coming Home to Self: The Adopted Child Grows Up.* Baltimore: Gateway Press, 2003.

Verrier, Nancy Newton. *The Primal Wound: Understanding the Adopted Child.* Baltimore: Gateway Press, 1993.

Acknowledgements

Writing *Adopted* has been a long journey for both of us, separately and together. We would not have made it this far without the input and support of some very special people.

A number of professionals in the adoption space both influenced and inspired us, as well as several therapists, counsellors, coaches, colleagues and authors who have played a part in helping us understand and heal from many of the issues that we, as adopted people, have faced. Particular thanks to Marilyn Morgan, Roy Bowden, Paul Bailey, Janet Milner, Margaret Musson, Elizabeth Stevens, Janetta Whalley, Lynley Brophy, Loretta Brown, Vivienne Hill, Susan Goldstiver and Nancy Verrier.

To our parents, three of whom passed away before this book could be completed, for your willingness to be interviewed, and in some cases to have your personal stories shared with others. Heartfelt thanks to Keith and Noeline, Sue, Tony, Jan, Bob, Tex and Helen.

To our friends and whānau who have assisted the work in various ways by reading versions of the manuscript, giving us honest, insightful and loving feedback, proofing every line, and providing a safe haven for reunion. Our deepest gratitude to Debbie, Trish, Margaret, Prue, Trevor, Julie, Leigh, Sally, Debra, Tamela, Jenny and Philip.

This book would likely never have reached such a broad audience without the team at Massey University Press. Our heartfelt thanks for your expert support, advice and professionalism. We are particularly grateful to Nicola Legat for believing in this project, and for the skilful and patient editing and guidance provided by Jude Watson, Tracey Borgfeldt and Anna Bowbyes. It's been an absolute privilege and pleasure to work with you.

Finally, we truly appreciate the openness so many adopted people, birth families and adoptive families we have met over the years have shown us in sharing their stories, heartaches and triumphs. We want to particularly acknowledge two special people who inspired us to keep going when the journey almost became too hard: thank you Liz and Genevieve.

About the authors

Jo Willis is an adopted person and a specialist in the field of adoption counselling, coaching and education. She is viewed as a leader in personal development within the adoption field. As an adolescent, she lobbied local and national politicians for amendments to be made to the 1955 Adoption Act. At the age of 21 she was reunited with her birth family prior to the change in legislation. Jo then became part of the implementation of the 1985 Adult Adoption Information Act, leading to a 24-year career as a social worker, senior practitioner and supervisor. Jo has worked in all facets of adoption and adult-adoption information social work practice in New Zealand.

She has also worked as a senior advisor in organisational development for the Ministry of Social Development, and consults to the ministry as a leadership consultant, as well as coaching participants on the Massey University (NZ) MA Advanced Leadership and EMBA programmes. She holds an MA in Coaching and Mentoring Practice (Oxford Brookes University, Oxford, UK), a Diploma in Counselling, and is an accredited member of the International Coaching Federation and NZ Positive Psychology Association.

Jo is a leadership and personal development coach who also

works with adopted adults to support them to understand and integrate their adoptive experience. Through counselling, coaching and mentoring, she helps those who feel confined by, or languishing in, adoption-related patterns to grow and flourish. Jo offers adopted people a personalised process along with evidence-based tools and resources to enhance the connection and belonging within themselves, leading to more ease in their relationships and life. She also coaches adopted leaders to increase their leadership impact and educates professionals about the impact of adoption on adopted people.

Jo lives in Napier with her husband Lawrie. Their son, Will, lives in Australia with his wife, Jasmine, and their children, Jack and Evie. Their daughter, Hollie, her husband, Cameron, and their son Hugo, live in Napier.

Jo's family and her work are her deepest fulfilment. Being a lifelong learner, she continues to grow and develop personally and spiritually. Regular yoga, walking and cycling enhance her wellbeing and her love of travel; watching movies, dancing, listening to podcasts and music keep her spirit young.

For further information see: www.jowilliscoach.com.

●

Brigitta Baker was adopted during the closed adoption era, and has been in reunion with her birth family since 2008. Her professional experience ranges from advisory roles in the public sector through to positions with large corporations within human resource management, training facilitation, leadership development, organisational development and coaching. Alongside her day job as a senior leader, Brigitta is training in psychotherapy with the aim of working more deeply with adopted people to help them process their experiences.

Writing has always been a key passion in her life. From the moment she had her first article published in a historical journal at the age of 17, Brigitta knew she had an affinity with the written word. A degree in history and sociology at Canterbury University meant that she did almost nothing but write for four years during her university studies. Since then, she has been the go-to person in every organisation she has worked for when marketing materials, website content, policy manuals, press releases, business plans and newsletters need to be written. She was never quite sure she had a book in her, and the process of writing *Adopted* has proved as challenging as everyone told her it would be.

Brigitta is based in Wellington with her husband, Andrew. Her two daughters, Zoë and Jade, are pursuing studies in Dunedin. She enjoys keeping fit by tackling the nearby hills and bush tracks, practising yoga on a regular basis, and walking their pampered puppy Molly around the waterfront. She occasionally has a bash around the tennis court with Andrew when he deigns to give her a lesson, but it often ends in tears as she doesn't like being told what to do (even by a former professional tennis coach)!

MASSEY
UNIVERSITY
PRESS

First published in 2022 by Massey University Press
Private Bag 102904, North Shore Mail Centre
Auckland 0745, New Zealand
www.masseypress.ac.nz

Text copyright © Brigitta Baker and Jo Willis, 2022
Images copyright © Brigitta Baker and Jo Willis, 2022

Design by Carolyn Lewis
Cover photographs copyright © Brigitta Baker (front)
and Jo Willis (back)

The moral rights of the authors have been asserted

All rights reserved. Except as provided by the Copyright
Act 1994, no part of this book may be reproduced, stored
in or introduced into a retrieval system or transmitted
in any form or by any means (electronic, mechanical,
photocopying, recording or otherwise) without the prior
written permission of both the copyright owner(s) and
the publisher.

A catalogue record for this book is available from the
National Library of New Zealand

Printed and bound in China by 1010 Printing Asia Ltd

ISBN: 978-1-99-101610-2
eISBN: 978-1-99-101611-9